JAPANESE HIRAGANA AND KATAKANA MADE EASY

An Easy Step-by-Step Workbook to Learn the Japanese Writing System

Lingo Mastery

ISBN: 978-1-951949-51-8

Contents

FREE BOOK REVEALS THE 6-STEP BLUEPRINT THAT TOOK STUDENTS FROM LANGUAGE LEARNERS TO FLUENT IN 3 MONTHS

Preface / About Japan

If you are reading this book, it's clear that you are thinking about learning Japanese and its writing system. We assure you that this book is an excellent choice.

Even though Japanese is known as one of the most difficult languages to learn, it is also one of the most popular languages. There are a number of reasons why there's a growing interest in learning Japanese. Many Japanese language learners first become interested in studying the language because of pop culture media such as manga, anime and video games. It's likely you have already encountered a Japanese anime show or played a game made by a Japanese company. If you learn to read and understand Japanese, it will open up the way for you to explore and enjoy all forms of pop culture in their original form.

For some people, another reason to learn Japanese is that it can expand their career opportunities. Although Japan is a relatively small country located in the far east of Asia, Japanese is spoken by more than 125 million people. It ranks number 9 on the list of the most spoken languages in the world. Also, since Japan has the third largest economy in the world, billions of dollars are spent each year by Japanese consumers. Surely then, learning Japanese would give you more opportunities in the business world—whether you are a company leader looking to expand into a new market or an employee exploring new job prospects.

Whatever your reasons are for choosing to learn Japanese, we want to assure you that you have chosen wisely. Japanese is an extremely useful language and it will definitely expand your worldview. This book, *Japanese Hiragana and Katakana Made Easy*, has been carefully designed to help new learners such as yourself learn hiragana and katakana in the fastest and most effective way possible, by providing fun exercises. This book will help you not only memorize each character but will also teach you vocabulary that is used in real-life situations with native Japanese speakers. As an added bonus, you will master clear pronunciation and a natural accent with the use of the supplementary audio recordings.

Together, let's start your journey of learning Japanese!

Introduction / About the Japanese Language

There are three sets of characters in Japanese: hiragana, katakana and kanji. They are often used together even in a single sentence and they all have a different role. Take a look at the example below.

ジョンは日本語を勉強しています。　John studies Japanese.

The words underlined with one stroke like this:＿are hiragana. The words underlined with two strokes like this:＿are katakana. The words underlined with the squiggle stroke like this:　are kanji. How are all three character sets used? Let's look at the roles of each character set.

Hiragana (ひらがな)

Hiragana is a phonetic alphabetic system that is mainly used for native Japanese words, conjugating verbs, and grammatical particles. A total of 46 hiragana characters is used in the Japanese writing system. The hiragana characters were developed based on simplified kanji (Chinese characters) in the beginning of the 9th century. For example, the hiragana character "あ" is a simplification of the Chinese character "安." Once you have memorized all the hiragana characters, you will know all of the possible sounds in the language.

Katakana (カタカナ)

Katakana is also a phonetic alphabetic system. It has 46 corresponding characters to the same sound in hiragana. But instead, it is used for loanwords and foreign names. The katakana characters were also developed based on the Chinese characters, but they were created by taking elements of Chinese characters. For example, this is a Chinese character "伊", and one part of this Chinese character was used to make this katakana character "イ."

Kanji (漢字)

Kanji are actually Chinese characters that were introduced to Japan back when the Japanese language did not yet have its own writing system. The kanji characters represent both meanings and sounds and they are mainly used for nouns and verbs. All Japanese students are required to learn 2,131 kanji characters by the time they graduate high school. These kanji characters are called the "joyo kanji" which means "commonly used kanji."

We suggest that you learn hiragana first, then katakana and finally kanji. This may sound intimidating right now but don't worry! This book will guide you step by step through hiragana and katakana. Feel free to read at your own pace and go back and review at any time. Hiragana will help you learn the proper Japanese pronunciation. Katakana will help you to read, for example, a menu at a restaurant, the names of electronic devices and the name of countries. Katakana will also help you to write your own name in Japanese.

How to Use this Book

This book, *Japanese Hiragana and Katakana Made Easy* will help you master all the hiragana and katakana characters over the course of 7 different lessons. The first 3 lessons focus only on hiragana. You will learn all 46 hiragana characters and how to write some basic words in Japanese. After you complete the first three lessons, you will not only be able to recognize each individual character, but you will also be able to pronounce it properly. There are fun exercises included as well for additional practice and memory retention.

The next three lessons focus on katakana. You will learn all of the 46 katakana characters and when to use them, since some words should be written in katakana only instead of hiragana. You will practice how to write some words, such as the names of countries, sports and electronic devices, in katakana.

All of the exercises are very practical so feel free to use the phrases you learn when you visit Japan or when you talk to your Japanese friends.

Finally, in lesson 7, you will learn some basic Japanese grammar and will practice how to introduce yourself in Japanese. At the end of this lesson, you should be able to write not only your name in Japanese, but also some simple sentences!

HOW TO GET THE AUDIO FILES

Some of the excercises throughout this book comes with accompanying audio files.

You can download these audio files if you head over to

www.LingoMastery.com/japanese-hk-audio

だい　　　しょう
第1章
LESSON 1

ひらがな
THE 46 HIRAGANA CHARACTERS

もくひょう Objective
- ⊘ Learn how to read and write all of the 46 basic hiragana characters.
- ⊘ Learn how to write the names of common items in hiragana.

まなぶこと Lesson Overview

Part 1: Hiragana Chart

Part 2: Practice

Reading and Writing
Practice 1
Practice 2

Listening and Speaking
Practice 1
Practice 2

Part 3 : Vocabulary

List of Japanese Vocabulary

Part 1: Hiragana Chart

ひらがなのよみかた
How to read hiragana 📢

Look at the chart below. You will see all 46 hiragana characters and the corresponding letters of the alphabet which is called "Romaji" in Japan. Listen to the audio and repeat. Pay careful attention to the pronunciation of each character.

See page 4 for audio.

あ	い	う	え	お
a	i	u	e	o
か	き	く	け	こ
ka	ki	ku	ke	ko
さ	し	す	せ	そ
sa	shi	su	se	so
た	ち	つ	て	と
ta	chi	tsu	te	to
な	に	ぬ	ね	の
na	ni	nu	ne	no
は	ひ	ふ	へ	ほ
ha (wa)	hi	fu	he (e)	ho
ま	み	む	め	も
ma	mi	mu	me	mo

や		ゆ		よ
ya		yu		yo
ら	り	る	れ	ろ
ra	ri	ru	re	ro
わ				を
wa				wo
ん				
n				

Part 2: れんしゅう Practice

Reading and Writing

The Japanese people consider their writing system to be an art form. This can be seen in the Japanese calligraphy called shodō (書道). We encourage you to pay careful attention to the order in which you write each character.

Japanese children practice Japanese calligraphy under the supervision of a calligraphy teacher.

There are three fundamental ways to finish a hiragana stroke. The hiragana character け (ke) has all three kinds of strokes, namely jump, stop and brushes. Some hiragana characters have only one kind of stroke and some have two kinds of strokes. When you practice writing the hiragana characters, pay attention not only to the stroke order but also which stroke finish you are supposed to use.

To explain what the different stroke finishes look like, we are going to use the character け (ke).

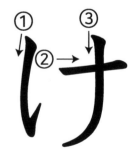

1. Jump (はねる): To write this character we start the stroke from the top to the bottom. At the end of the stroke, you create a check mark effect then change direction to where stroke number 2 begins.

2. Stop (とめる): As shown by the image on the right, you begin writing stroke number 2 from left to right and complete it when you get to the red dot.

3. Brushes (はらう): For stroke number 3, start from the top then slowly move down, create a slight bend and then make a sharp point.

Practice 1: ひらがなをれんしゅうしよう。
Practice writing hiragana.

① あ〜お

	Romaji	Stroke Order		
あ	a	一	た	あ

あ	あ	あ	あ	あ	あ

	Romaji	Stroke Order	
い	i	し	い

い	い	い	い	い	い

	Romaji	Stroke Order
① → ② → う	u	` ＼ ｜ う

う	う	う	う	う	う

	Romaji	Stroke Order
① → ② → え	e	` ＼ ｜ え

え	え	え	え	え	え

	Romaji	Stroke Order		
お	。	一	お	お

お　お　お　お　お　お

② か～こ

	Romaji	Stroke Order		
か	ka	つ	カ	か

か　か　か　か　か　か

	Romaji	Stroke Order			
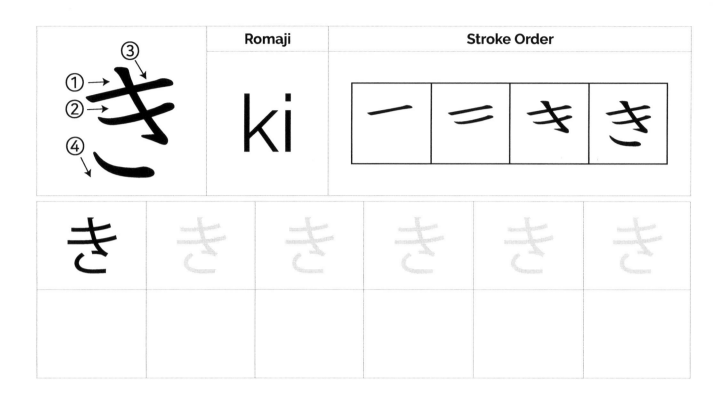 き ① ② ③ ④	ki	一	二	き	き

き	き	き	き	き	き

	Romaji	Stroke Order
く ①	ku	く

く	く	く	く	く	く

	Romaji	Stroke Order	
け ① ② ③	ke	し | し- | け	

け け け け け け

	Romaji	Stroke Order	
こ ① ②	ko	丶 | こ	

こ こ こ こ こ こ

③ さ～そ

	Romaji	Stroke Order		
さ	sa	一	十	さ

さ	さ	さ	さ	さ	さ

	Romaji	Stroke Order
し	shi	し

し	し	し	し	し	し

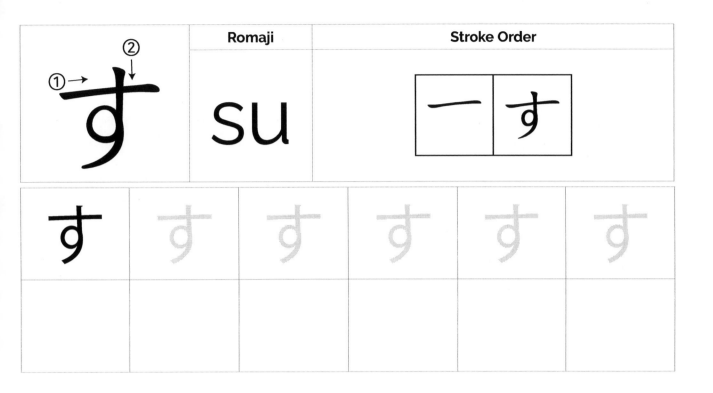

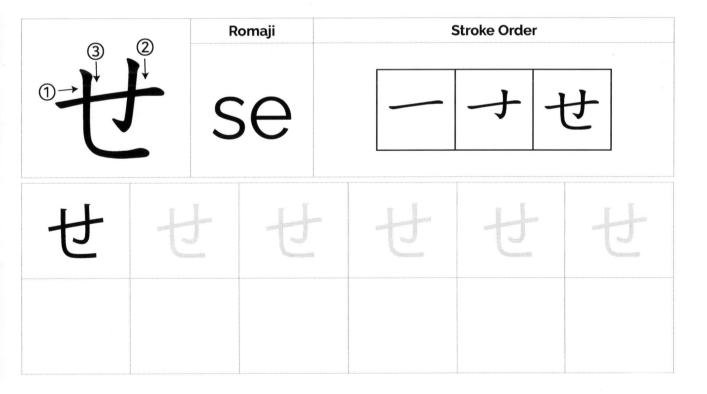

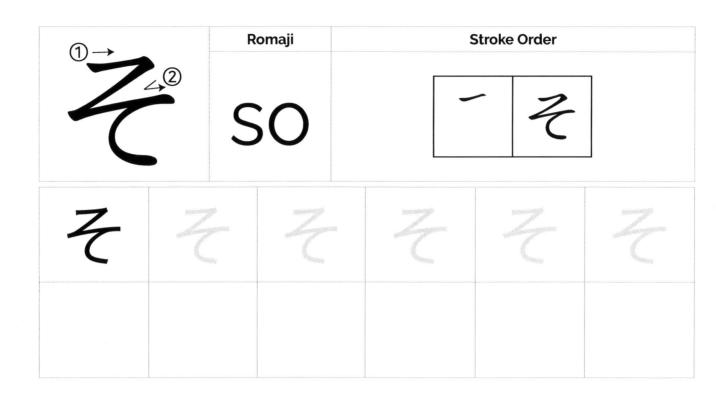

	Romaji	Stroke Order
そ	so	ー そ

そ	そ	そ	そ	そ	そ

④   た〜と

	Romaji	Stroke Order
た	ta	ー ナ た た

た	た	た	た	た	た

	Romaji	Stroke Order
① → ち ②	chi	一 ち

ち	ち	ち	ち	ち	ち

	Romaji	Stroke Order
① → つ	tsu	つ

つ	つ	つ	つ	つ	つ

	Romaji	Stroke Order
① て	te	て

て	て	て	て	て	て	て

	Romaji	Stroke Order
① ② と	to	' | と

と	と	と	と	と	と

⑤ な〜の

	Romaji	Stroke Order			
な	na	一	ナ	ナ	な

な		な	な	な	な	な

	Romaji	Stroke Order		
に	ni	い	に	に

に		に	に	に	に	に

	Romaji	Stroke Order
ぬ ① ②	nu	し | ぬ

ぬ ぬ ぬ ぬ ぬ ぬ

	Romaji	Stroke Order
ね ① ②	ne	ﾉ | ね

ね ね ね ね ね ね

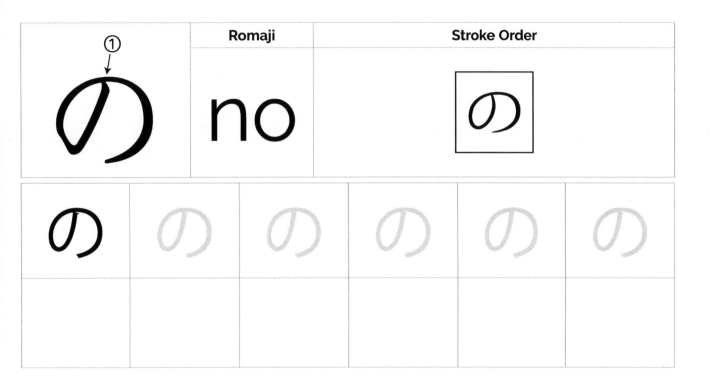

	Romaji	Stroke Order
の	no	の
の	の	の	の	の	の

⑥ は～ほ

	Romaji	Stroke Order
は	ha (wa)	I I- は
は	は	は	は	は	は

	Romaji	Stroke Order
① ひ	hi	ひ

ひ	ひ	ひ	ひ	ひ	ひ

	Romaji	Stroke Order			
① ② ③ ④ ふ	fu	`	ろ	ふ	ふ

ふ	ふ	ふ	ふ	ふ	ふ

	Romaji	Stroke Order
へ	he (e)	へ

へ	へ	へ	へ	へ	へ

	Romaji	Stroke Order			
ほ	ho	し	し	に	ほ

ほ	ほ	ほ	ほ	ほ	ほ

	Romaji	Stroke Order		
① → **ま** ③ ↓ ② →	ma	一	二	ま

ま	ま	ま	ま	ま	ま

	Romaji	Stroke Order	
① → **み** ② ↓	mi	み	み

み	み	み	み	み	み

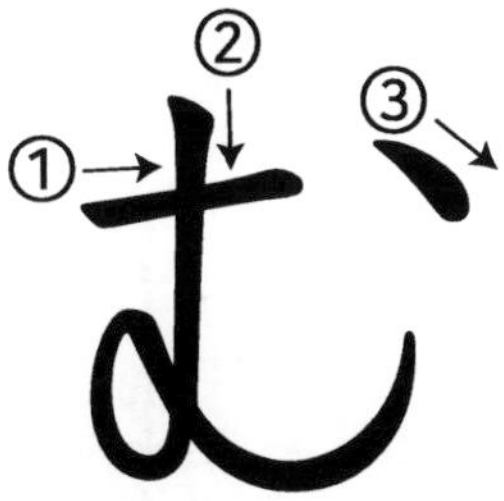

	Romaji	Stroke Order
む ① → ② ③	mu	一 も む

む む む む む む

	Romaji	Stroke Order
め ① ②	me	ヽ め

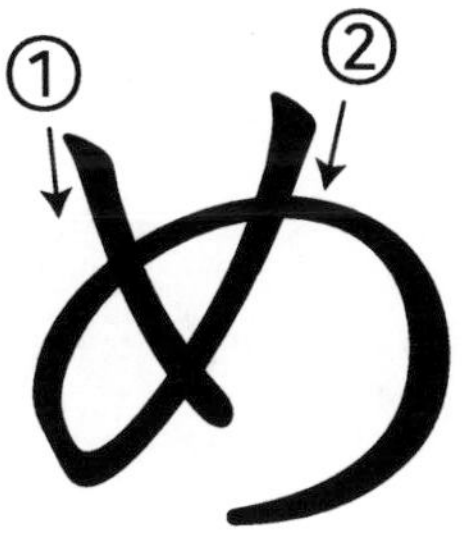

め め め め め め

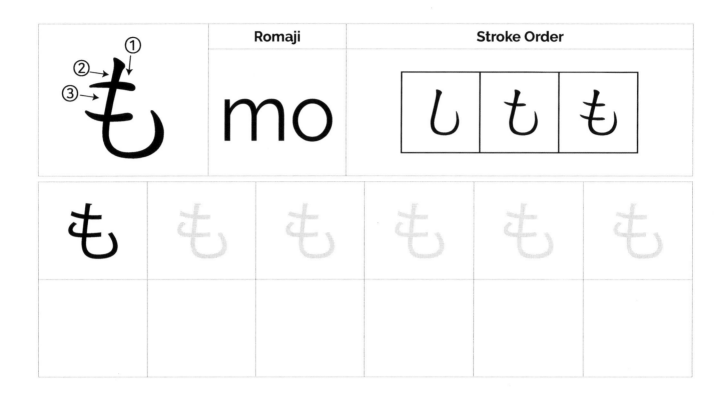

	Romaji	Stroke Order		
も	mo	し	も	も

も | も | も | も | も | も

⑧　や～よ

	Romaji	Stroke Order		
や	ya	っ	や	や

や | や | や | や | や | や

	Romaji	Stroke Order
① ② ゆ	yu	ロ ゆ

ゆ	ゆ	ゆ	ゆ	ゆ	ゆ

	Romaji	Stroke Order
② ① よ	yo	- よ

よ	よ	よ	よ	よ	よ

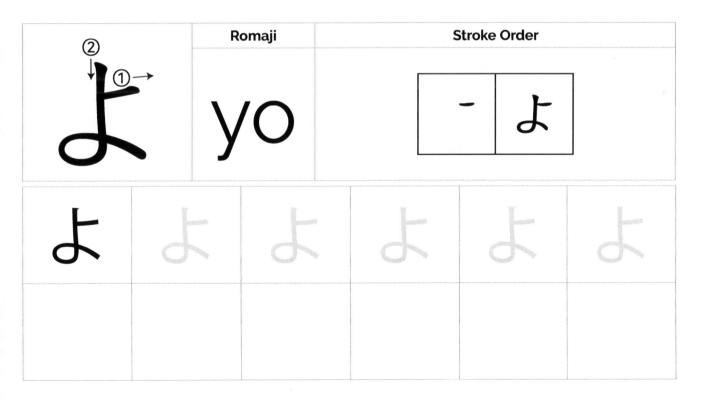

⑨　ら～ろ

	Romaji	Stroke Order
ら	ra	` ` ` ら `

ら	ら	ら	ら	ら	ら

	Romaji	Stroke Order
り	ri	` い ` ` り `

り	り	り	り	り	り

	Romaji	Stroke Order
① → る	ru	る

る	る	る	る	る	る

	Romaji	Stroke Order
① ② → れ	re	Ｊ　れ

れ	れ	れ	れ	れ	れ

	Romaji	Stroke Order
① → **ろ**	ro	ろ

ろ	ろ	ろ	ろ	ろ	ろ

⑩ わ～ん

	Romaji	Stroke Order
② → **わ** ①↓	wa	J わ

わ	わ	わ	わ	わ	わ

	Romaji	Stroke Order
を	WO	一　ナ　を
を	を	を	を	を	を

	Romaji	Stroke Order
ん	n	ん
ん	ん	ん	ん	ん	ん

Practice 2: ただしいひらがなをえらぼう。
Select the correct hiragana character.

1）**Ka:** ①あ   ②か   ③わ   ④く   ⑤き
2）**Mo:** ①ま   ②も   ③け   ④し   ⑤み
3）**Shi:** ①そ   ②さ   ③り   ④も   ⑤し
4）**Tsu:** ①つ   ②し   ③ら   ④よ   ⑤こ
5）**Te:** ①た   ②ふ   ③て   ④を   ⑤ろ
6）**Ne:** ①な   ②ぬ   ③の   ④ね   ⑤れ
7）**No:** ①る   ②や   ③ゆ   ④の   ⑤こ
8）**Re:** ①り   ②れ   ③わ   ④す   ⑤た
9）**So:** ①し   ②ん   ③そ   ④う   ⑤え
10）**Wo:** ①あ   ②ち   ③を   ④く   ⑤わ

11）**Ki:** ①き   ②し   ③り   ④ち   ⑤ひ
12）**Nu:** ①ふ   ②う   ③ぬ   ④の   ⑤ろ
13）**Ra:** ①よ   ②か   ③た   ④や   ⑤ら
14）**To:** ①お   ②ろ   ③と   ④こ   ⑤ぬ
15）**Fu:** ①は   ②ふ   ③へ   ④な   ⑤ん
16）**Chi:** ①さ   ②す   ③ら   ④ち   ⑤た
17）**Ya:** ①か   ②に   ③き   ④し   ⑤や
18）**Se:** ①せ   ②お   ③え   ④そ   ⑤と
19）**Ku:** ①く   ②へ   ③つ   ④ん   ⑤お
20）**Ho:** ①は   ②ほ   ③け   ④そ   ⑤ろ

Listening and Speaking

In this part of the exercise, multiple audio recordings have been prepared. Listen carefully to all the audio recordings to practice your listening skills.

Practice 1: おんせいをきいて、たんごをえらぼう。📢

Listen to the audio and choose the correct word.

See page 4 for audio.

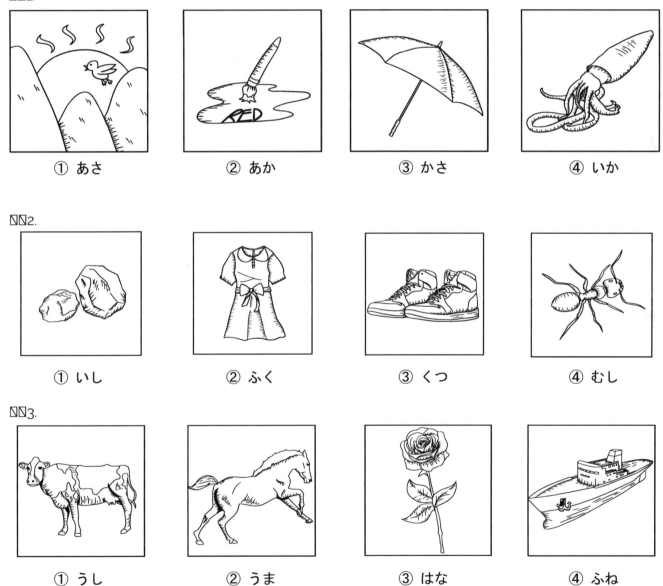

1.

① あさ   ② あか   ③ かさ   ④ いか

2.

① いし   ② ふく   ③ くつ   ④ むし

3.

① うし   ② うま   ③ はな   ④ ふね

4.

① あめ   ② かめ   ③ すし   ④ さめ

5.

① まち   ② みち   ③ ゆき   ④ ほし

6.

① とけい   ② おかね   ③ くるま   ④ おとこ

7.

① やま   ② ゆめ   ③ かわ   ④ おんな

Practice 2: たんごをききとって、かいてみよう。

Listen to the audio and write down what you hear in the box.
See page 4 for audio.

1. Sun

2. Hot

3. Cold

4. Moon

5. Night

6. Mandarin orange

◻◻

7. Subway

8. Train Station

9. Airport

10. Police Officer

11. Japan

Part 3: Vocabulary

In this part of the lesson, you will learn new Japanese vocabulary. All the vocabulary can be written in hiragana. This lesson will test your hiragana writing skills.

Practice 1: みぢかなものをにほんごでかいてみよう。
Look carefully at each item in the picture and write the name of each item in Japanese.

①	**hasami / scissors**		⑥	**e / drawing**
②	**saifu / wallet**		⑦	**isu / chair**
③	**okashi / sweets**		⑧	**kami / paper**
④	**osara / plate**		⑨	**hon / book**
⑤	**tokei / clock**		⑩	**tsukue / desk**

たんごリスト：List of Japanese Vocabulary

This is all the vocabulary you have learned in this lesson:

あさ：morning
あか：red
かさ：umbrella
いか：squid
いし：stone
ふく：clothes
くつ：shoes
むし：bug
うし：cow
うま：horse
はな：flower
ふね：ship
あめ：rain
かめ：turtle
すし：sushi
さめ：shark
まち：town
みち：road, way
ゆき：snow
ほし：star
とけい：clock
おかね：money
くるま：car
おとこ：man
やま：mountain
ゆめ：dream
かわ：river
おんな：woman
たいよう：sun
あつい：hot
さむい：cold
つき：moon
よる：night
にもつ：baggage

ちかてつ：subway
えき：station
くうこう：airport
けいさつ：police
にほん：Japan
はさみ：scissors
さいふ：wallet
おかし：sweets
おさら：plate
え：drawing
いす：chair
かみ：paper
ほん：book
つくえ：desk

第2章
だい　　　　しょう

LESSON 2

<ruby>濁点<rt>だくてん</rt></ruby>と<ruby>半濁点<rt>はんだくてん</rt></ruby>

濁点と半濁点
HIRAGANA WITH DIACRITICAL MARKS

もくひょう　Objective

- ✔ Learn how to read and write additional Japanese sounds using diacritical marks.
- ✔ Learn how to write the names of body parts and days of the week in Japanese.

まなぶこと　Lesson Overview

Part 1: Hiragana with Diacritical Marks (chart)

Part 2: Practice

Reading and Writing
Practice 1
Practice 2

Listening and Speaking
Practice 1
Practice 2

Part 3: Vocabulary

Part 4: Greeting in Japanese

List of Japanese Vocabulary

Part 1: Hiragana with Diacritical Marks

Look at the chart below. You will see all 25 hiragana characters with diacritical marks and the corresponding letters of the alphabet. Pay careful attention to the pronunciation of each character. Listen to the audio and repeat. 📢

が	ぎ	ぐ	げ	ご
ga	gi	gu	ge	go
ざ	じ	ず	ぜ	ぞ
za	ji	zu	ze	zo
だ	ぢ	づ	で	ど
da	ji[*1]	zu[*2]	de	do
ば	び	ぶ	べ	ぼ
ba	bi	bu	be	bo
ぱ	ぴ	ぷ	ぺ	ぽ
pa	pi	pu	pe	po

*1 じ (ji) and ぢ (ji) sound the same. *2 ず (zu) and づ (zu) sound the same.

The two small dashes (゛) are called *dakuten* (濁点) or *tenten*. The small circle (゜) is called *handakuten* (半濁点) or *maru*. By adding these diacritical marks onto the hiragana characters, you can change the sound of the character. The chart below shows how diacritical marks change the sounds of hiragana characters.

	か	き	く	け	こ
K	ka	ki	ku	ke	ko
	が	ぎ	ぐ	げ	ご
G	ga	gi	gu	ge	go

Keeping in mind the chart above, here is another chart that has letters that follow the same pattern. With the *dakuten* (゛), the consonants *k, s, t, h* become the consonants *g, z, d, b*, respectively. The sound of voiced consonants is stronger and comes from the throat, and you should feel a puff of air when you say it. The consonant *h* changes to a *p* sound with *handakuten* (゜).

K゛	→	G
S゛	→	Z
T゛	→	D
H゛	→	B
H゜	→	P

Part 2: れんしゅう Practice

Reading and Writing

As you write each hiragana character with *dakuten* and *handakuten*, read it aloud. Pay close attention to the stroke order and trace the light gray characters. Then follow the same pattern to form the hiragana characters in the blank boxes provided below.

Practice 1: れんしゅうしよう.

Practice writing hiragana with diacritical marks. Below you will find words that consist of hiragana characters with diacritical marks.

1. が (ga)

ga i ko tsu / skeleton

ma n **ga** / Japanese comics

me **ga** ne / eyeglasses

ga ka / painter

2. ぎ（gi）

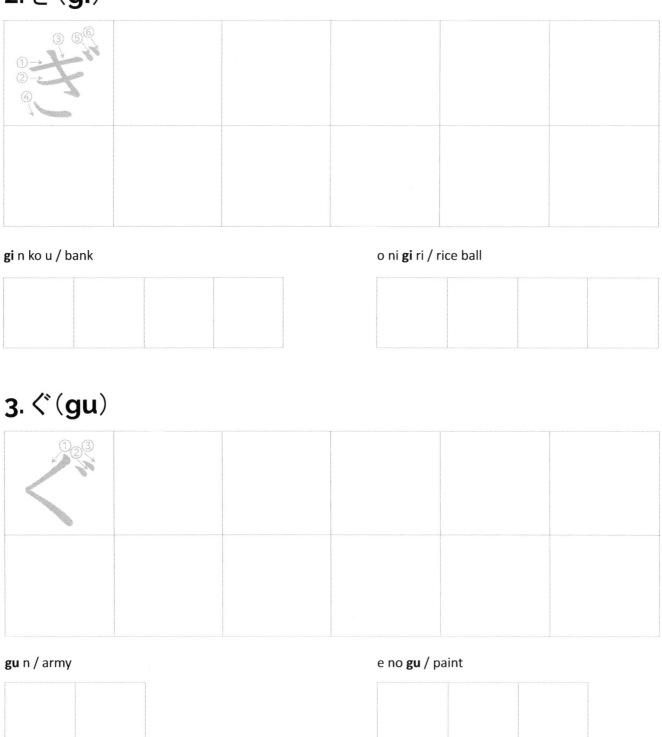

gi n ko u / bank

o ni gi ri / rice ball

3. ぐ（gu）

gu n / army

e no gu / paint

4. げ (ge)

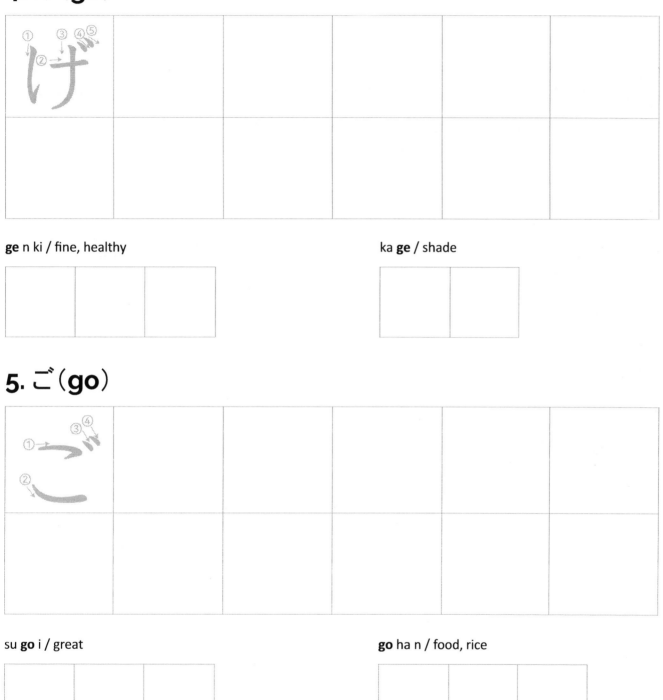

ge n ki / fine, healthy

ka **ge** / shade

5. ご (go)

su **go** i / great

go ha n / food, rice

6. ざ (za)

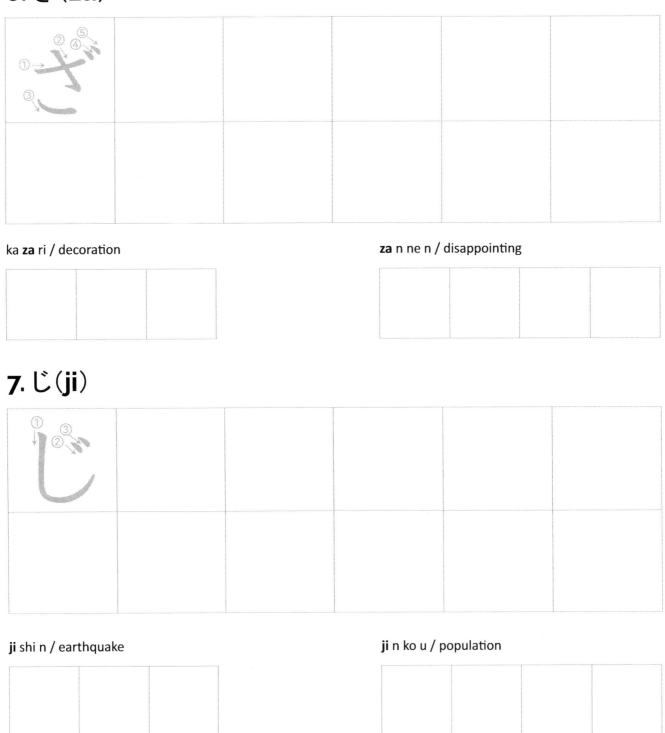

ka **za** ri / decoration

za n ne n / disappointing

7. じ (ji)

ji shi n / earthquake

ji n ko u / population

8. ず (zu)

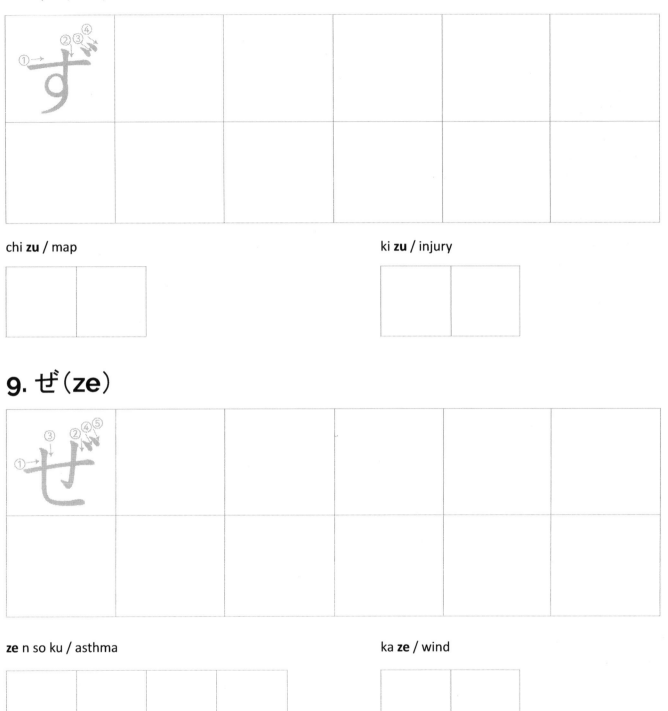

chi **zu** / map

ki **zu** / injury

9. ぜ (ze)

ze n so ku / asthma

ka **ze** / wind

10. ぞ (zo)

ka **zo** ku / family

na **zo** / riddle

11. だ (da)

da i ko n / Japanese radish

da n **da** n / gradually

12. ぢ (ji)

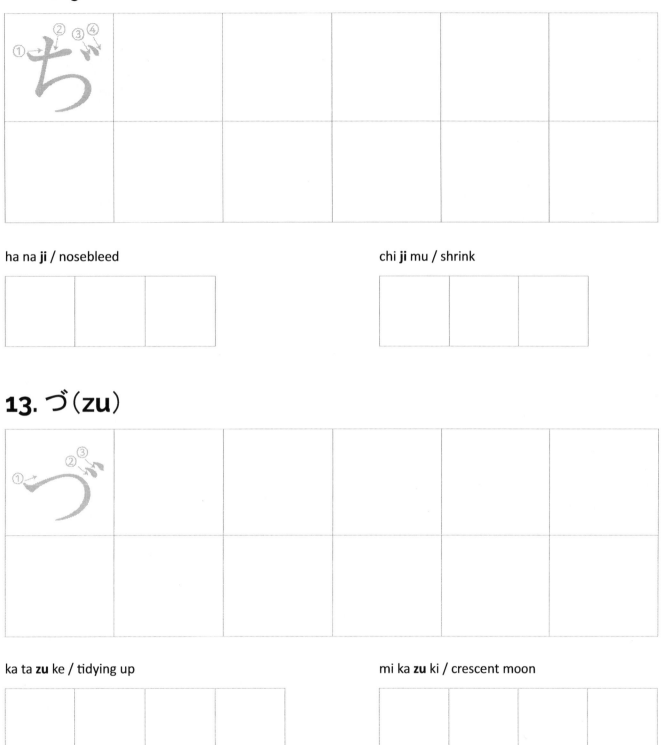

ha na **ji** / nosebleed

chi **ji** mu / shrink

13. づ (zu)

ka ta **zu** ke / tidying up

mi ka **zu** ki / crescent moon

14. で (de)

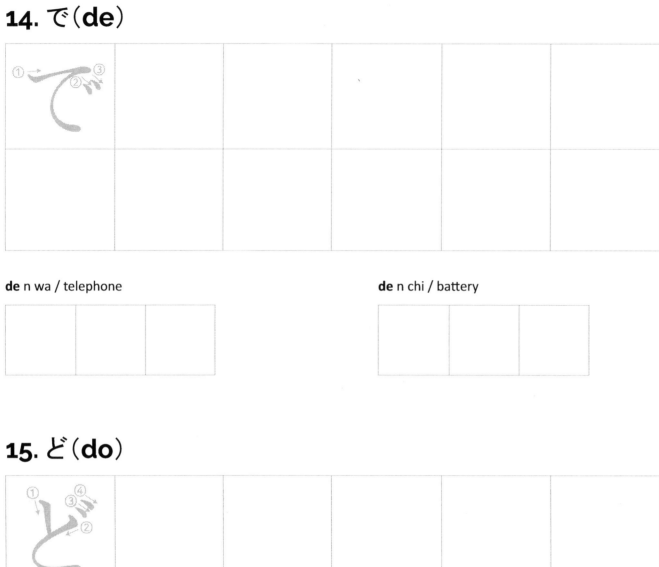

de n wa / telephone

de n chi / battery

15. ど (do)

ma do / window

do ro / mud

16. ば (ba)

so **ba** / soba (Japanese noodles)

ba ra / rose

17. び (bi)

ka **bi** / mold

bi ji n / beautiful woman

18. ぶ (bu)

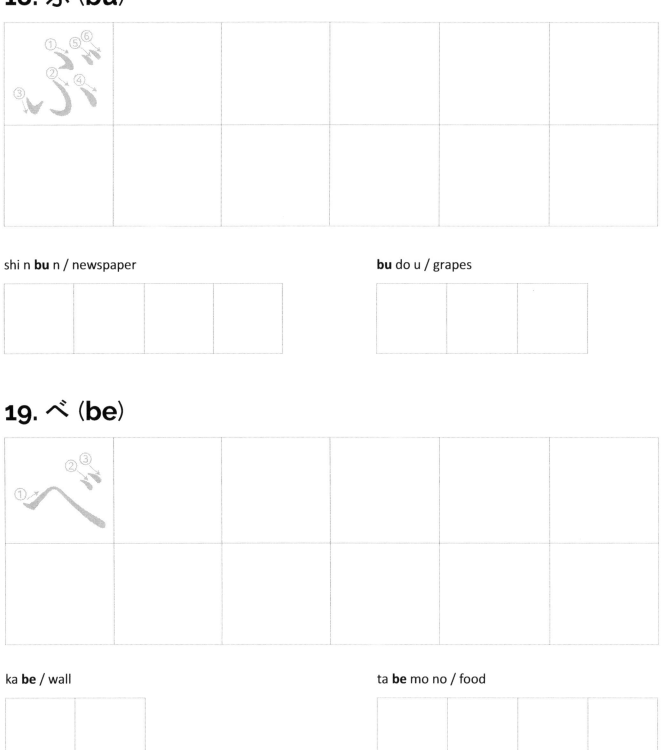

shi n **bu** n / newspaper

bu do u / grapes

19. べ (be)

ka **be** / wall

ta **be** mo no / food

20. ぼ (bo)

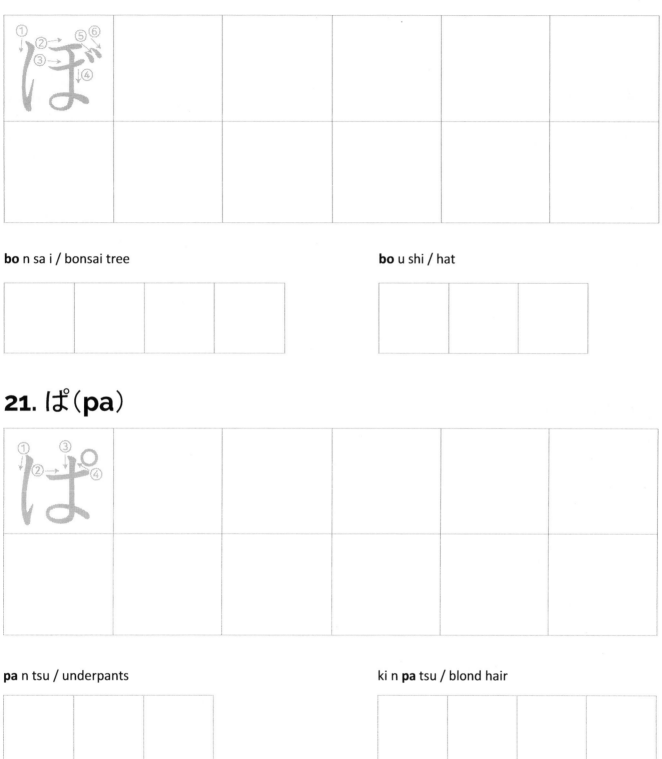

bo n sa i / bonsai tree

bo u shi / hat

21. ぱ (pa)

pa n tsu / underpants

ki n **pa** tsu / blond hair

22. ぴ (pi)

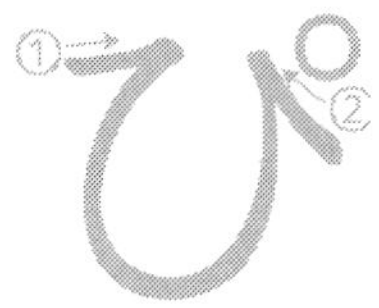

pi ka **pi** ka / sparkle

e n **pi** tsu / pencil

23. ぷ (pu)

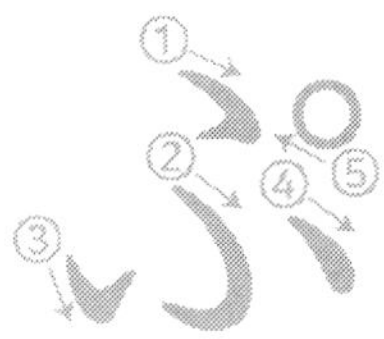

te n **pu** ra / tempura

pu ri n / custard pudding

24. ぺ (pe)

pe ri ka n / pelican

pe n gi n / penguin

25. ぽ (po)

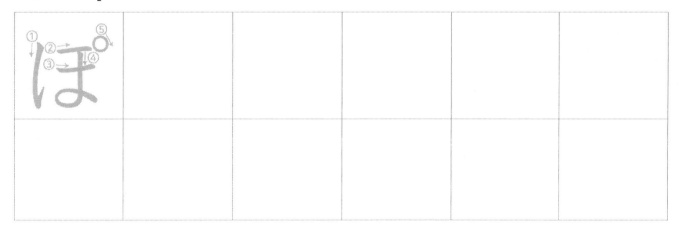

sa n **po** / walk

shi n **po** / progress

Practice 2: ただしいひらがなをえらぼう。
Choose the correct hiragana character.

1) Gi: ①じ　②ぢ　③び　④ご　⑤ぎ

2) Za: ①ざ　②だ　③ば　④ぜ　⑤じ

3) De: ①ぜ　②で　③べ　④ぺ　⑤ぞ

4) Bu: ①づ　②ぐ　③ぶ　④ぷ　⑤げ

5) Pe: ①ぱ　②ぷ　③ぽ　④ぺ　⑤で

6) Gu: ①ぐ　②ご　③ど　④ぼ　⑤ず

7) Ze: ①で　②ぱ　③ぴ　④び　⑤ぜ

8) Do: ①び　②が　③ど　④ざ　⑤ば

9) Pu: ①ず　②ご　③ぴ　④ぷ　⑤ぱ

10) Ga: ①じ　②が　④ざ　⑤ぼ　⑥ぺ

Practice 3: ようびをにほんごでいってみよう。
Trace the light gray characters in the boxes below and read the words out loud.

1) Monday	5) Friday
げ　つ　よ　う　び	き　ん　よ　う　び

2) Tuesday	6) Saturday
か　よ　う　び	ど　よ　う　び

3) Wednesday	7) Sunday
す　い　よ　う　び	に　ち　よ　う　び

4) Thursday	
も　く　よ　う　び	

Listening and Speaking

Practice 1: おんせいをきいて、たんごをえらぼう。📢
Listen to the audio and choose the correct word.

1.

①ふで　　　　②そば　　　　③げた　　　　④かぎ

2.

①かぶき　　　　②おじぎ　　　　③はがき　　　　④そうじ

3.

①でんわ　　　　②でんき　　　　③かんじ　　　　④じかん

4.

①ゆび   ②たび   ③みず   ④くじ

5.

①しんでん   ②しんぶん   ③かんでん   ④ごうかく

6.

①おりがみ   ②ふじさん   ③おじさん   ④どろぼう

7.

①えんぴつ   ②ぴんぽん   ③せんぱい   ④はんざい

Practice 2: たんごをききとって、かいてみよう。📢

Listen to the audio and write down what you hear in the boxes below.

1. Animal

2. Music

3. College, university

4. Lawyer

5. Busy

Part 3: Vocabulary

Practice 1: からだのなまえをかいてみよう。

Fill in the boxes with the name of the corresponding body part.

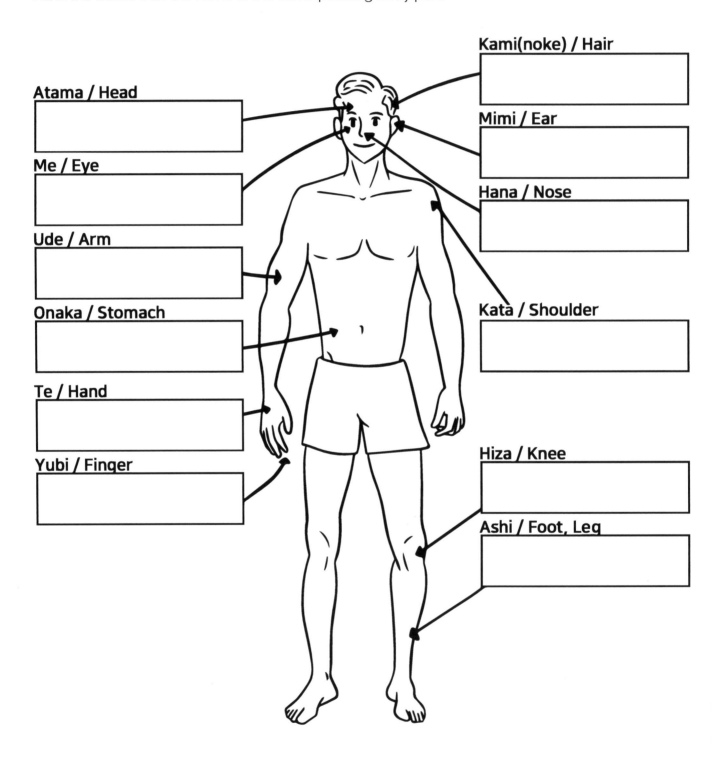

Atama / Head

Me / Eye

Ude / Arm

Onaka / Stomach

Te / Hand

Yubi / Finger

Kami(noke) / Hair

Mimi / Ear

Hana / Nose

Kata / Shoulder

Hiza / Knee

Ashi / Foot, Leg

Part 4: Greetings

Practice 1: にほんごであいさつしてみよう。📢
Listen to the audio and repeat.

おはよう。	Good morning.
おはようございます。	Good morning. (Polite)
こんにちは。	Good afternoon.
こんばんは。	Good evening.
さようなら。	Goodbye.
おやすみ。	Good night.
ありがとう。	Thank you.
ありがとうございます。	Thank you very much. (Polite)
すみません。	Excuse me. / I'm sorry.
ただいま。	I'm home.
おかえりなさい。	Welcome home.
いただきます。	Let's eat.
ごちそうさまでした。	Thank you for the meal. (After eating)
はじめまして。	Nice to meet you.
よろしくおねがいします。	Thank you in advance.

Helpful tips!

すみません : This expression is mainly used in two ways. The first way you can use it is: "Excuse me" to get someone's attention. The second way you can use it is: "I'm sorry" (polite) to apologize for a mistake or for an inconvenience.

いただきます : Japanese people use this expression before they eat something. The direct translation would be "I humbly receive." This expression originally comes from Japan's roots in Buddhism. By saying this phrase, they express their gratitude for all living things including plants, animals and farmers. It is a way to show gratitude for everyone involved in cultivating, preparing and cooking the meal before you.

よろしくおねがいします : Japanese people use this expression in various situations. It can be translated as "Thank you for your continued help," "Thank you in advance" or "I look forward to working with you." One of the most common ways to use this expression is when you ask your co-worker, business partner or customer to do something. At the end of your request, you can say it, meaning: "Thank you in advance." You can also use it after you introduce yourself for the first time to your clients, classmates or co-workers, meaning: "I'm looking forward to working with you."

Practice 2: きこえたあいさつをかいてみよう。📢
Listen to the audio and write what you hear.

1)
2)
3)
4)
5)

Practice 3: ただしいあいさつをしよう。

In the following situations what greeting would be more appropriate to use?

1) You come to the classroom in the morning and greet your classmates.

2) It is 7 o'clock at night. You happen to meet your teacher on the street.

3) You arrived late for a meeting.

4) You are going to start eating the meal you prepared.

6) You ask your business partner to do something and you want to thank him in advance.

たんごリスト：List of Japanese Vocabulary

This is all the vocabulary you have learned in this lesson:

がいこつ：skeleton
がか：painter
めがね：eyeglasses
まんが：manga
ぎんこう：bank
おりがみ：origami
ぐん：army
えのぐ：paint
げんき：fine, healthy
かげ：shade
すごい：great
ごはん：food, rice
かざり：decoration
ざんねん：disappointing
じしん：earthquake
じんこう：population
ちず：map
きず：injury
ぜんそく：asthma
かぜ：wind
かぞく：family
なぞ：riddle
だいこん：Japanese radish
だんだん：gradually
はなぢ：nosebleed
ちぢむ：shrink
かたづけ：tidying up
みかづき：crescent moon
でんわ：telephone
でんち：battery
まど：window

どろ：mud
そば：soba
ばら：rose
かび：mold
びじん：beautiful woman
しんぶん：newspaper
ぶどう：grape
かべ：wall
たべもの：food
ぼんさい：bonsai
ぼうし：hat
ぱんつ：underpants
きんぱつ：blond hair
ぴかぴか：sparkle
えんぴつ：pencil
てんぷら：tempura
ぷりん：custard pudding
ぺりかん：pelican
ぺんぎん：penguin
さんぽ：walk
しんぽ：progress
げつようび：Monday
かようび：Tuesday
すいようび：Wednesday
もくようび：Thursday
きんようび：Friday
どようび：Saturday
にちようび：Sunday
かぎ：key
おじぎ：bow
でんき：electricity

みず：water
どろぼう：thief
どうぶつ：animal
おんがく：music
だいがく：university
べんごし：lawyer
いそがしい：busy
あたま：head
め：eye
うで：arm
おなか：stomach
て：hand
ゆび：finger
かみ（のけ）：hair
みみ：ear
はな：nose
かた：shoulder
ひざ：knee
あし：foot, leg

だい　　　しょう

第3章

LESSON 3

拗音と促音

ようおん　そくおん

CONTRACTED SOUNDS AND DOUBLE CONSONANTS

もくひょう　Objective

- ✓ Learn how to read and write contracted sounds and double consonants.
- ✓ Learn how to write the names of animals and family members.
- ✓ Learn how to ask the questions "Where is…?" and "How much is…?"

まなぶこと　Lesson Overview

Part 1: Contracted sounds and double consonants

Part 2: Practice

Reading and Writing
Practice 1
Practice 2
Practice 3

Listening and Speaking
Practice 1
Practice 2

Part 3 : Vocabulary

Part 4 : Where is…?

Part 5 : Numbers and Price

List of Japanese Vocabulary

Part 1: Contracted Sounds and Double Consonants

1) Contracted Sounds 📢

The small や、ゆ and よ are used to transcribe contracted sounds. You will see all hiragana characters with the small や、ゆ and よ. Listen to the audio and repeat. Pay careful attention to the pronunciation of each character.

きゃ	きゅ	きょ
kya	kyu	kyo
しゃ	しゅ	しょ
sha	shu	sho
ちゃ	ちゅ	ちょ
cha	chu	cho
にゃ	にゅ	にょ
nya	nyu	nyo
ひゃ	ひゅ	ひょ
hya	hyu	hyo
みゃ	みゅ	みょ
mya	myu	myo
りゃ	りゅ	りょ
rya	ryu	ryo

ぎゃ	ぎゅ	ぎょ
gya	gyu	gyo
じゃ	じゅ	じょ
ja	ju	jo

びゃ	びゅ	びょ
bya	byu	byo
ぴゃ	ぴゅ	ぴょ
pya	pyu	pyo

2) Double Consonants (Small "tsu") 📢

The small letter つ is used when transcribing double consonants such as *tt* and *pp*. See the example below. Listen carefully to the audio and repeat.

はっぱ (happa)   leaf
ざっし (zasshi)   magazine
あさって (asatte)   day after tomorrow

きって (kitte)   stamp
ちょっと (chotto)   a little bit
さっぽろ (Sapporo)   name of a city

Part 2: れんしゅう Practice

Reading and Writing

As you write each hiragana character with the small や、ゆ and よ, read it aloud. Pay close attention to the stroke order and trace the light gray characters in the first box. Then practice writing them without the guide in the blank boxes.

Practice 1: れんしゅうしよう。

Practice writing hiragana with the small letters.

1) Kya

2) Kyu

3) Kyo

4) Sha

5) Shu

し ゆ

6) Sho

し よ

7) Cha

ち や

8) Chu

ち ゆ

9) Cho

ち よ

10) Nya

にや

11) Nyu

にゆ

12) Nyo

によ

13) Hya

ひや

14) Hyu

ひゆ

15) Hyo

ひょ

16) Mya

みゃ

17) Myu

みゅ

18) Myo

みょ

19) Rya

りゃ

20) Ryu

りゅ

21) Ryo

りょ

22) Gya

ぎゃ

23) Gyu

ぎゅ

24) Gyo

ぎょ

25) Ja

じゃ

26) Ju

じゅ

27) Jo

じょ

28) Bya

びゃ

29) Byu

びゅ

30) Byo

び ょ

31) Pya

ぴ ゃ

32) Pyu

ぴ ゅ

33) Pyo

ぴ ょ

Practice 2: ただしいひらがなをえらぼう。
Select the correct hiragana character.

1) Myu:	①きゃ	②ぎゃ	③みゅ	④しゅ	⑤にゅ
2) Pyu:	①しゃ	②ぴゅ	③ぎゃ	④びゅ	⑤びょ
3) Kyo:	①ちゃ	②にゃ	③しゃ	④きょ	⑤ぴゃ
4) Gya:	①ぎゃ	②びょ	③ひょ	④きゃ	⑤ぴゅ
5) Bya:	①きょ	②びゃ	③りゃ	④ひゃ	⑤みゃ
6) Hya:	①ちゅ	②ちゃ	③ひゃ	④りょ	⑤じょ
7) Sha:	①ぎょ	②しゃ	③きょ	④じゃ	⑤じゅ
8) Nya:	①ちょ	②ちゃ	③びゃ	④びゅ	⑤にゃ
9) Kya:	①ぴゅ	②じゅ	③きゅ	④きゃ	⑤ひょ
10) Jo:	①じゅ	②しゅ	③じょ	④にゃ	⑤りゃ

Practice 3: ことばをかいてみよう。
Fill in the boxes with hiragana characters.

Shu ku da i / Homework

O **cha** / Tea

Mo ku **hyo** u / Goal

Ya **kyu** u / Baseball

Ju gyo u / Class, lesson

Ki **ppu** / Ticket

Listening and Speaking

Practice 1: おんせいをきいて、たんごをえらぼう.📢
Listen to the audio and choose the correct word.

1. ①こんしゅう   ②せんしゅう   ③らいしゅう   ④しゅうかい
2. ①きって   ②ざっし   ③ばった   ④きっぷ
3. ①かいしゃ   ②でんしゃ   ③りょくちゃ   ④いしゃ
4. ①ぎゅうにゅう   ②きょうりゅう   ③れんしゅう   ④ふくしゅう
5. ①うちゅう   ②よしゅう   ③こしょう   ④きゅうり

Practice 2: たんごをききとって、かいてみよう.📢
Listen to the audio and write down what you hear in the box.

1. Soy sauce

2. Potato

3. Locust

4. Goldfish

5. Tokyo

6. Pumpkin

7. Cucumber

8. Brother

9. Picture

Part 3: Vocabulary

Practice 1: どうぶつのなまえをかいてみよう。

Write the animal names in hiragana.

①	Tori (Bird)		⑦	Neko (Cat)	
②	Kujaku (Peacock)		⑧	Kaeru (Frog)	
③	Hyou (Leopard)		⑨	Hebi (Snake)	
④	Kuma (Bear)		⑩	Uma (Horse)	
⑤	Inu (Dog)		⑪	Ushi (Cow)	
⑥	Nezumi (Rat)		⑫	Saru (Monkey)	

Practice 2: かぞくのよびかたをおぼえよう。
Learn family terms.

Now let's learn how to address your family members. There are formal terms and informal terms to address members of your own family. You can use the formal term when you are speaking about your family in a formal situation, for example in a job interview. However, when you are speaking about somebody else's family, you have to use a different term to refer to them. For families other than your own, use the terms in the category "Someone else's family" to refer to them. You can use informal terms when you are speaking to your family or when you are speaking about your family in a casual situation.

Below are the terms for family members. Read them aloud to practice pronunciation. 📣

English	Formal	Informal	Someone else's family
Father	ちち	おとうさん	おとうさん
Mother	はは	おかあさん	おかあさん
Older brother	あに	おにいちゃん	おにいさん
Older sister	あね	おねえちゃん	おねえさん
Younger brother	おとうと	おとうと	おとうとさん
Younger sister	いもうと	いもうと	いもうとさん
Grandfather	そふ	おじいちゃん	おじいさん
Grandmother	そぼ	おばあちゃん	おばあさん

Part 4: どこですか？ Where is...?

In this lesson, you will learn how to ask for a location when you travel. Pay close attention to the sentence below. *Doko* (どこ) is "where?" in English. You can simply add the name of the place you are looking for in the box to complete the sentence.

はどこですか?
(wa do ko de su ka)

Practice 1: ばしょのなまえをおぼえよう。📢

Listen to the audio and fill in the boxes with the name of each building.

①	Toshokan (Library)		⑤	Yuubinkyoku (Post Office)	
②	Gakkou (School)		⑥	Byouin (Hospital)	
③	Keisatsusho (Police Station)		⑦	Ryougaejo (Exchange)	
④	Ginkou (Bank)		⑧	Toire (Bathroom)	

Practice 2: ばしょをたずねてみよう。

Using the 8 different locations you learned in the previous activity, make 8 sentences with the question: where is...?

Locations	Where is....?
Library	
Police Station	
School	
Bank	
Post Office	
Hospital	
Exchange	
Bathroom	

Part 5: かずとねだん Numbers and Price

In this lesson, we will learn how to count in Japanese and how to ask the price for something. Pay close attention to the box below and pronounce each number.

Practice 1: おんせいをききながら、かずをはつおんしてみよう。📢

Listen to the audio and read aloud all the numbers in each box.

0	ぜろ／れい				
1	いち	11	じゅういち	30	さんじゅう
2	に	12	じゅうに	40	よんじゅう
3	さん	13	じゅうさん	50	ごじゅう
4	し／よん	14	じゅうし／じゅうよん	60	ろくじゅう
5	ご	15	じゅうご	70	ななじゅう
6	ろく	16	じゅうろく	80	はちじゅう
7	なな／しち	17	じゅうなな／じゅうしち	90	きゅうじゅう
8	はち	18	じゅうはち	100	ひゃく
9	きゅう／く	19	じゅうきゅう／じゅうく		
10	じゅう	20	にじゅう		

100	ひゃく	1000	せん	10000	いちまん
200	にひゃく	2000	にせん	20000	にまん
300	さんびゃく	3000	さんぜん	30000	さんまん
400	よんひゃく	4000	よんせん	40000	よんまん
500	ごひゃく	5000	ごせん	50000	ごまん
600	ろっぴゃく	6000	ろくせん	60000	ろくまん
700	ななひゃく	7000	ななせん	70000	ななまん
800	はっぴゃく	8000	はっせん	80000	はちまん
900	きゅうひゃく	9000	きゅうせん	90000	きゅうまん

Practice 2: おんせいをきいて、きこえたかずをかこう。📢

Listen to the audio and write the numbers you heard.

①		⑥	
②		⑦	
③		⑧	
④		⑨	
⑤		⑩	

If you want to ask the price at the store, you can simply say これはいくら ですか? (Kore wa ikura desu ka?). This phrase means "How much is this?" But you can also be more specific by adding the name of the product at the beginning of the sentence. In this case you replace これ which means "this" with the name of the product.

ko no
この 　　　　　　　　　　

wa i ku ra de su ka
はいくらですか?

How much is this...?

The official currency of Japan is the 円 (yen), which is pronounced *en* in Japanese. As of July 2021, 1 U.S. dollar is worth approximately 110 yen.

Practice 3: おんせいをきいて、くうはくをうめよう。📢

Listen to the audio and fill in the blank spaces. Choose an item from pictures below.

（　　　　）円です。

この（　　　　）はいくらですか?

1. A: この（　　　　　　　）はいくらですか？
    B: （　　　　　）円です。

2. A: この（　　　　　　　）はいくらですか？
    B: （　　　　　）円です。

3. A: この（　　　　　　　）はいくらですか？
    B: （　　　　　）円です。

4. A: この（　　　　　　　）はいくらですか？
    B: （　　　　　）円です。

5. A: この（　　　　　　　）はいくらですか？
    B: （　　　　　）です。

6. A: この（　　　　　　　）はいくらですか？
    B: （　　　　　）円です。

Items

たんごリスト： **List of Japanese Vocabulary**
This is all the vocabulary you have learned in this lesson:

はっぱ：leaf
ざっし：magazine
あさって：the day after tomorrow
きって：stamp
ちょっと：a little bit
さっぽろ：Sapporo (name of a city)
しゅくだい：homework
やきゅう：baseball
おちゃ：tea
じゅぎょう：class, lesson
もくひょう：goal
らいしゅう：next week
きっぷ：ticket
でんしゃ：train
れんしゅう：practice
うちゅう：universe
しょうゆ：soy sauce
じゃがいも：potato
ばった：locust
きんぎょ：goldfish
とうきょう：Tokyo
かぼちゃ：pumpkin
きゅうり：cucumber

きょうだい：brother
しゃしん：picture
とり：bird
ねこ：cat
くじゃく：peacock
かえる：frog
ひょう：leopard
へび：snake
くま：bear
うま：horse
いぬ：dog
うし：cow
ねずみ：rat, mouse
さる：monkey
としょかん：library
ゆうびんきょく：post office
がっこう：school
びょういん：hospital
けいさつしょ：police station
りょうがえじょ：exchange
ぎんこう：bank
といれ：bathroom

だい　　　しょう
第4章
LESSON 4

カタカナ
THE 46 KATAKANA CHARACTERS

もくひょう Objective
- Learn how to read and write all of the 46 basic katakana characters.

まなぶこと Lesson Overview

Part 1: Katakana Chart

Part 2: Practice

Reading and Writing
Practice 1
Practice 2
Practice 3

Listening and Speaking
Practice 1
Practice 2

List of Japanese Vocabulary

Part 1: Katakana Chart

カタカナのよみかた
How to read katakana 📢

Look at the chart below. You will see all 46 katakana characters and the corresponding letters of the alphabet. Listen to the audio and repeat. Pay careful attention to the pronunciation of each character.

ア	イ	ウ	エ	オ
a	i	u	e	o
カ	キ	ク	ケ	コ
ka	ki	ku	ke	ko
サ	シ	ス	セ	ソ
sa	shi	su	se	so
タ	チ	ツ	テ	ト
ta	chi	tsu	te	to
ナ	ニ	ヌ	ネ	ノ
na	ni	nu	ne	no
ハ	ヒ	フ	ヘ	ホ
ha (wa[1])	hi	fu	he (e)	ho
マ	ミ	ム	メ	モ
ma	mi	mu	me	mo

ヤ		ユ		ヨ
ya		yu		yo
ラ	リ	ル	レ	ロ
ra	ri	ru	re	ro
ワ				ヲ
wa				wo
ン				
n				

*1 ハ in katakana is rarely pronounced "wa."

The most common way to use katakana is for transcribing foreign words. Foreign names are transcribed to katakana: for example, John, Tom and Mike. If you are not Japanese, you will write your name using katakana instead of hiragana or kanji. However, after transcribing English words into katakana, the original pronunciation changes slightly because some sounds, such as those created by the letters (l and th) do not exist in Japanese. Later in this lesson, you will see an example of this (Practice 3).

Besides foreign words, katakana is often used for animal names, names of food, and company or brand names. Even Japanese words are sometimes written in katakana to emphasize the word. There are some examples below to illustrate.

1) Animal Names

The names of animals and plants species are commonly written in katakana. If the animal name is originally a foreign name such as ライオン (lion), it is written in katakana. In some cases, even if the name is in Japanese, it can also be written in katakana. You will notice this in the example below. The word for bear is 熊 (kuma) in Japanese. As illustrated in the example below, it can be written in kanji, hiragana or katakana and all are acceptable. There is no official rule on how to write animal or plant names.

Kanji	Hiragana	Katakana
熊	くま	クマ

2) Company Names

Katakana is often used for company or brand names. For example, the car manufacturer Toyota is written in katakana (トヨタ) instead of hiragana (とよた) even though it is a Japanese company.

Part 2: れんしゅう Practice

Reading and Writing

As you saw in the chart above, katakana characters are straight and angled while hiragana characters are curved and looping. Just as in hiragana, there are three fundamental ways to finish a katakana stroke. The katakana character オ (o) has all three kinds of strokes. Let's see a detailed example.

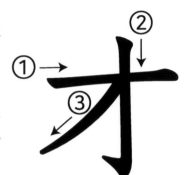

1. **Stop (とめる):** To write this character we start the stroke from the left to the right. You need to make a straight line similar to a minus sign (ー).

2. **Jump (はねる):** You start writing from the top to the bottom. At the end of the stroke, you create a check mark effect.

3. **Brushes (はらう):** Make a slanted and a shorter bar beginning from the cross point towards the bottom left. At the end of the stroke, you make a sharp point.

Paying careful attention to the stroke order and stroke finish are especially important since some of the katakana characters are quite similar. See the example below. Notice the differences between シ and ツ, or ソ and ン

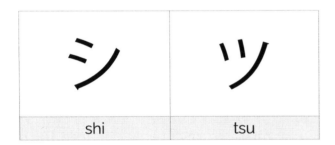

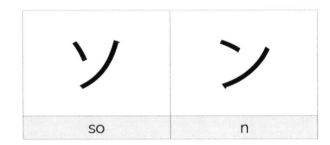

By carefully paying attention to stroke order of each katakana character and how you finish the stroke, each katakana character will stand out more clearly, thus minimizing confusion.

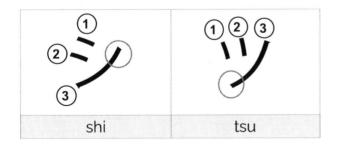

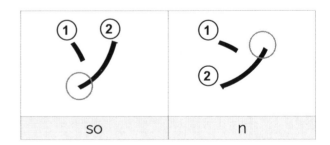

Practice 1: カタカナをれんしゅうしよう。

Practice writing katakana.

① 　ア〜オ

	Romaji	Stroke Order
①→ ア ②↓	a	㇆ ｜ ア

ア	ア	ア	ア	ア	ア

	Romaji	Stroke Order
① イ ②↓	i	ノ ｜ イ

イ	イ	イ	イ	イ	イ

	Romaji	Stroke Order
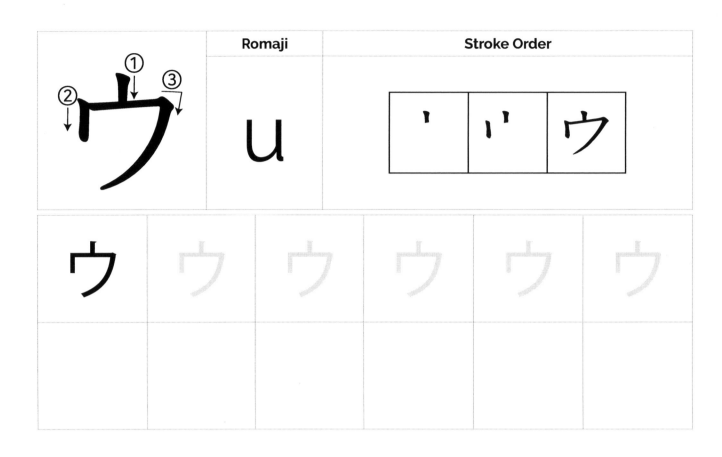

	Romaji	Stroke Order
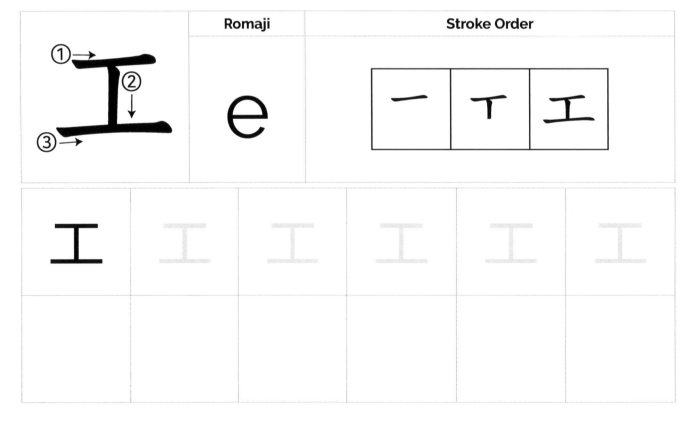

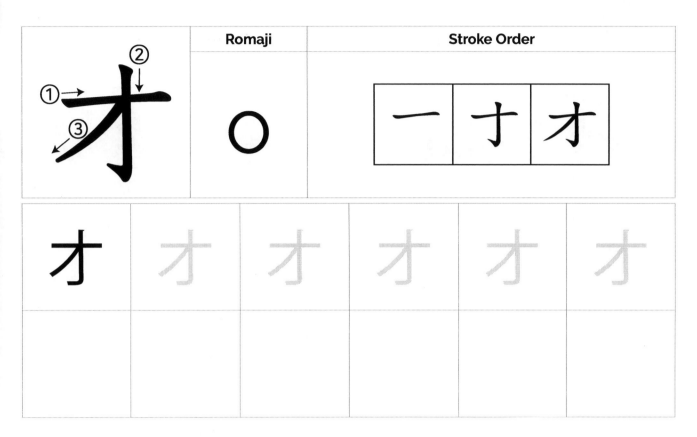

	Romaji	Stroke Order
オ	o	一 ナ オ

オ	オ	オ	オ	オ	オ

② カ〜コ

	Romaji	Stroke Order
力	ka	フ 力

力	力	力	力	力	力

	Romaji	Stroke Order
	ki	一 ニ キ

キ	キ	キ	キ	キ	キ

	Romaji	Stroke Order
	ku	ノ ク

ク	ク	ク	ク	ク	ク

	Romaji	Stroke Order
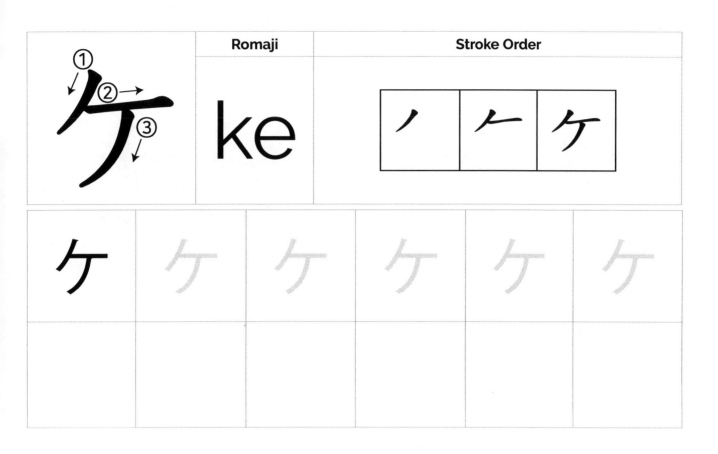	ke	ノ　ㇵ　ケ

ケ	ケ	ケ	ケ	ケ	ケ

	Romaji	Stroke Order
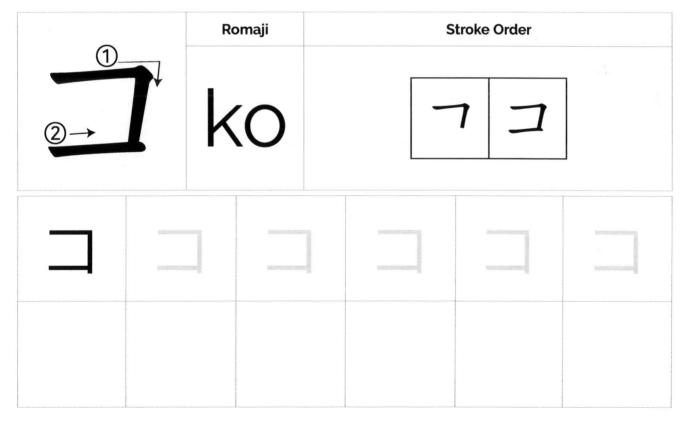	ko	コ　コ

コ	コ	コ	コ	コ	コ

③　サ〜ソ

	Romaji	Stroke Order		
サ	sa	一	十	サ

サ	サ	サ	サ	サ	サ

	Romaji	Stroke Order		
シ	shi	`丶`	`ﾉ`	シ

シ	シ	シ	シ	シ	シ

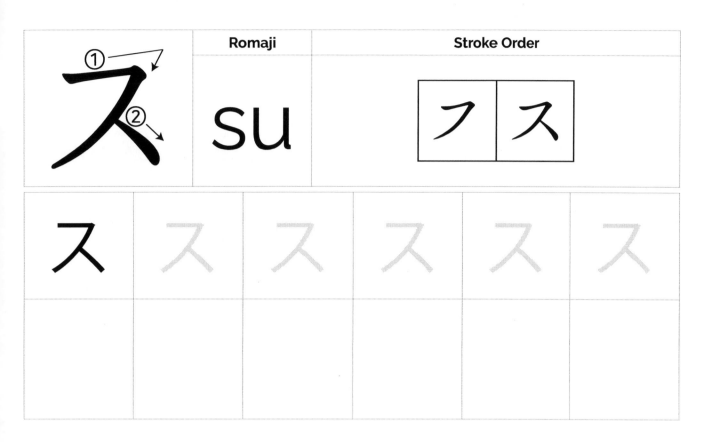

	Romaji	Stroke Order
ス	su	フ | ス

ス ス ス ス ス ス ス

	Romaji	Stroke Order
セ	se	⊃ | セ

セ セ セ セ セ セ セ

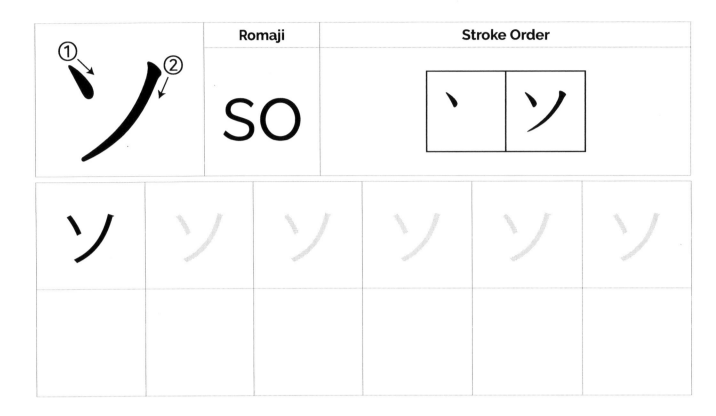

	Romaji	**Stroke Order**		
ソ	SO	`	ソ	

ソ	ソ	ソ	ソ	ソ	ソ

③　タ〜ト

	Romaji	**Stroke Order**		
タ	ta	ノ	ク	タ

タ	タ	タ	タ	タ	タ

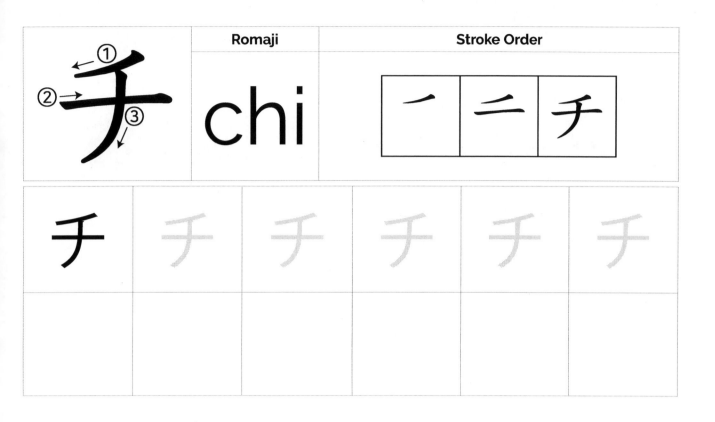

	Romaji	**Stroke Order**		
チ	chi	一	二	チ

チ チ チ チ チ チ チ

	Romaji	**Stroke Order**		
ツ	tsu	ヽ	ヽヽ	ツ

ツ ツ ツ ツ ツ ツ

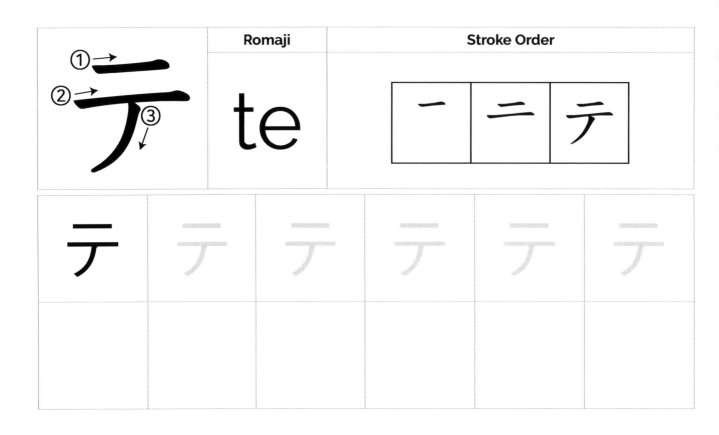

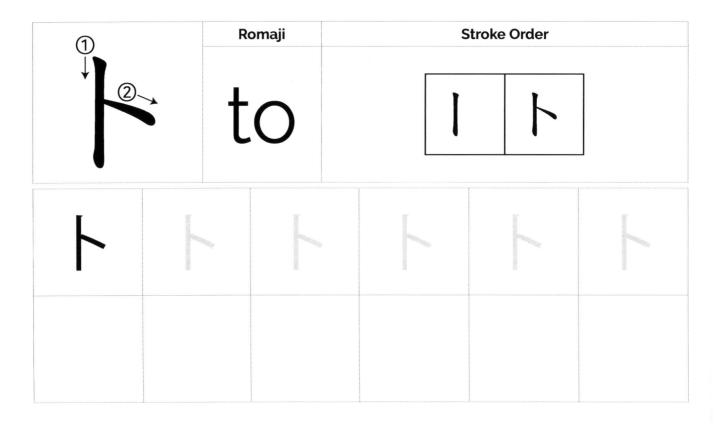

⑤　ナ〜ノ

	Romaji	Stroke Order	
ナ	na	一	ナ

ナ	ナ	ナ	ナ	ナ	ナ

	Romaji	Stroke Order	
ニ	ni	一	二

二	二	二	二	二	二

	Romaji	Stroke Order	
ヌ	nu	フ	ヌ

ヌ	ヌ	ヌ	ヌ	ヌ	ヌ	ヌ

	Romaji	Stroke Order			
ネ	ne	丶	ラ	ネ	ネ

ネ	ネ	ネ	ネ	ネ	ネ

	Romaji	Stroke Order
ノ ①	no	ノ

ノ	ノ	ノ	ノ	ノ	ノ

⑥ ハ〜ホ

	Romaji	Stroke Order
ハ ① ②	ha	ノ | ハ

ハ	ハ	ハ	ハ	ハ	ハ

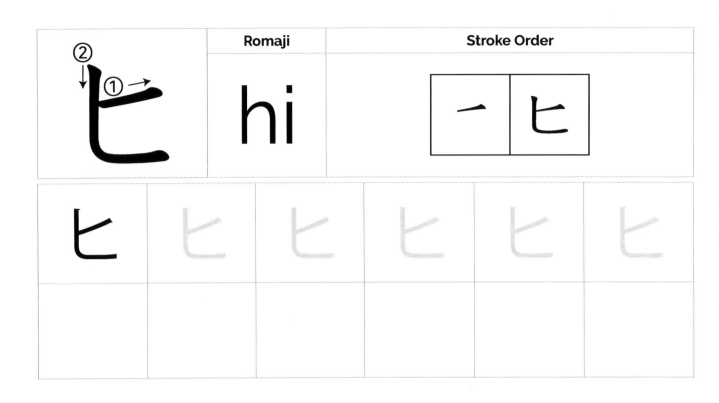

	Romaji	Stroke Order	
② ヒ ①	hi	一	ヒ
ヒ	ヒ	ヒ	ヒ	ヒ	ヒ	ヒ

	Romaji	Stroke Order
① フ	fu	フ
フ	フ	フ	フ	フ	フ	フ

	Romaji	Stroke Order

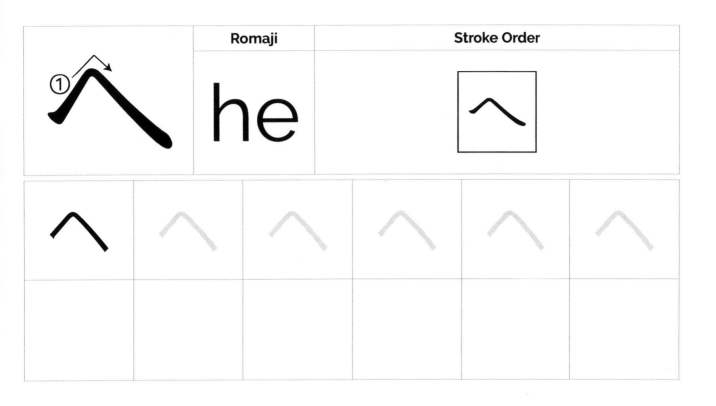

	Romaji	Stroke Order

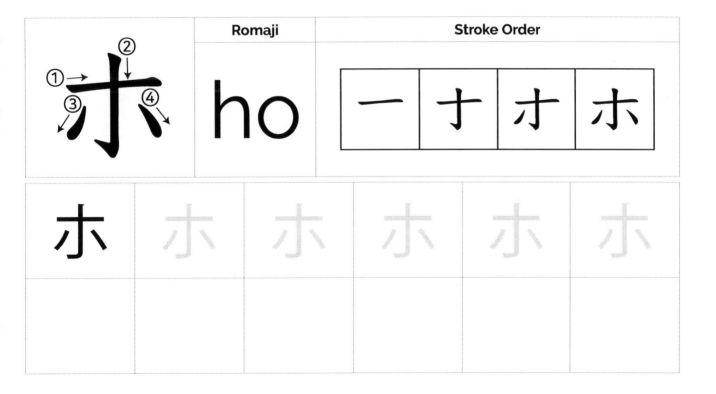

	Romaji	Stroke Order
① ② マ	ma	⁀ ⁀マ

マ	マ	マ	マ	マ	マ

	Romaji	Stroke Order
① ② ③ ミ	mi	ヽ ヾ ミ

ミ	ミ	ミ	ミ	ミ	ミ

	Romaji	Stroke Order
ム	mu	㇛ | ム

ム	ム	ム	ム	ム	ム

	Romaji	Stroke Order
メ	me	ノ | メ

メ	メ	メ	メ	メ	メ

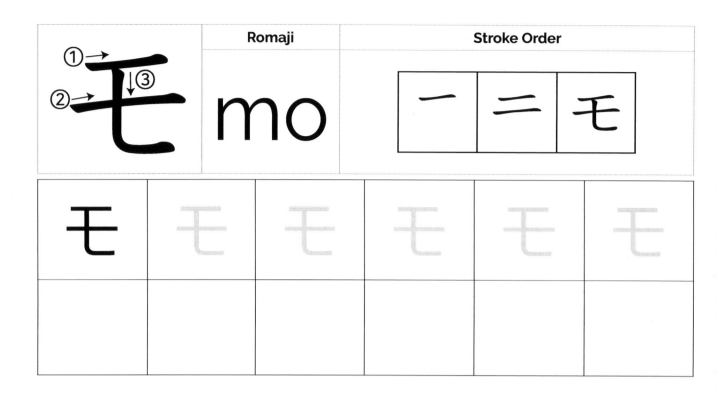

	Romaji	Stroke Order		
モ	mo	一	二	モ

モ	モ	モ	モ	モ	モ

⑧　ヤ〜ヨ

	Romaji	Stroke Order	
ヤ	ya	つ	ヤ

ヤ	ヤ	ヤ	ヤ	ヤ	ヤ

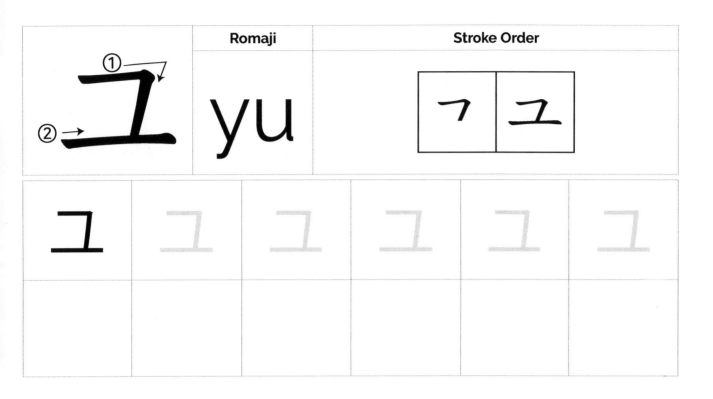

	Romaji	Stroke Order
ユ	yu	ㄱ　ユ

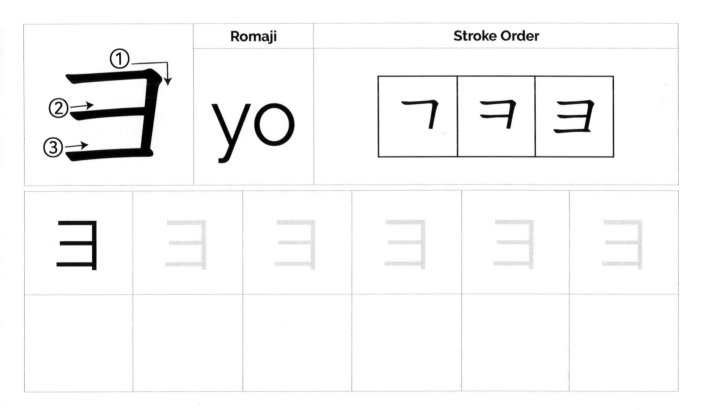

	Romaji	Stroke Order
ヨ	yo	ㄱ　ヲ　ヨ

	Romaji	Stroke Order	
①→ ②→ラ	ra	一	ラ

ラ	ラ	ラ	ラ	ラ	ラ

	Romaji	Stroke Order	
①↓　②↓ リ	ri	ｌ	リ

リ	リ	リ	リ	リ	リ

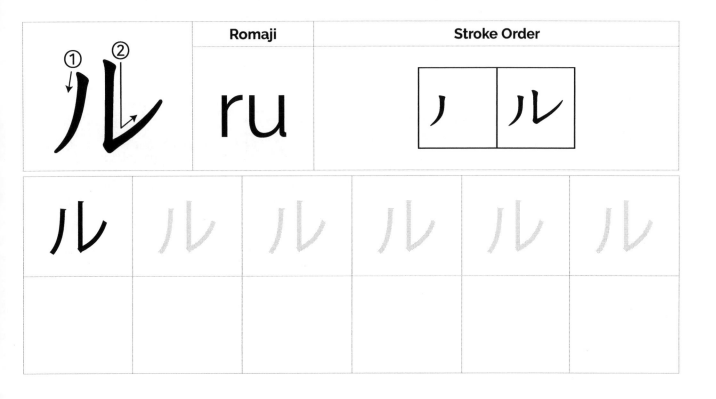

	Romaji	Stroke Order
ル① ②	ru	ノ | ル

ル	ル	ル	ル	ル	ル

	Romaji	Stroke Order
レ①	re	レ

レ	レ	レ	レ	レ	レ

	Romaji	Stroke Order
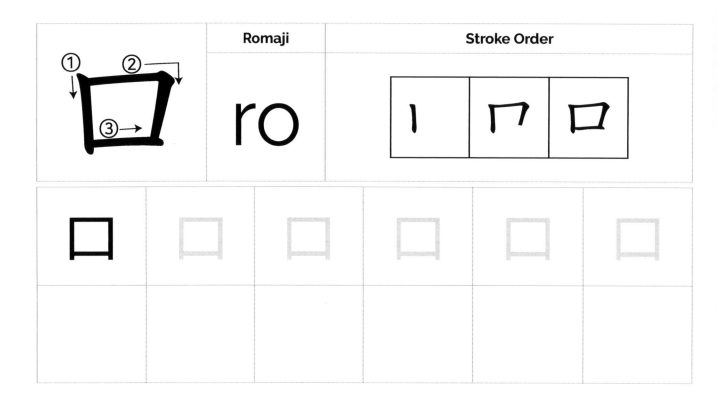 ro		ﺍ ﺍﺍ ﺍﺍﺍ

⑩　ワ〜ン

	Romaji	Stroke Order
	wa	ﺍ ﺍ

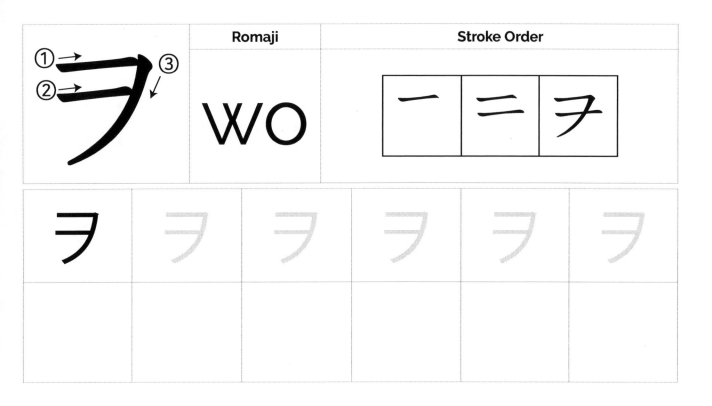

	Romaji	Stroke Order	
ヲ	WO	一 ニ ヲ	

ヲ　ヲ　ヲ　ヲ　ヲ　ヲ　ヲ

	Romaji	Stroke Order	
ン	n	丶 ン	

ン　ン　ン　ン　ン　ン

Practice 2: ただしいカタカナをえらぼう。
Select the correct katakana character.

1）**Ki:**　①イ　　②キ　　③チ　　④ツ　　⑤モ
2）**Sa:**　①モ　　②ヨ　　③サ　　④エ　　⑤ミ
3）**Te:**　①テ　　②ラ　　③ユ　　④ヲ　　⑤フ
4）**Na:**　①メ　　②ム　　③レ　　④ナ　　⑤ソ
5）**Ho:**　①モ　　②ロ　　③オ　　④ア　　⑤ホ
6）**Me:**　①マ　　②メ　　③ケ　　④レ　　⑤ワ
7）**Yo:**　①ヨ　　②ロ　　③コ　　④エ　　⑤タ
8）**Ra：**　①ヲ　　②ラ　　③ヨ　　④コ　　⑤ヤ
9）**Ke:**　①コ　　②セ　　③ネ　　④ケ　　⑤エ

10）**Su:**　①イ　　②チ　　③フ　　④メ　　⑤ス
11）**Tsu:**①シ　　②ミ　　③ツ　　④ヘ　　⑤ウ
12）**No:**　①ノ　　②メ　　③イ　　④ソ　　⑤ン
13）**Hi:**　①ウ　　②ト　　③ヒ　　④オ　　⑤マ
14）**Mo:**　①チ　　②ヨ　　③オ　　④モ　　⑤キ
15）**Ya**　①ク　　②シ　　③チ　　④カ　　⑤ヤ
16）**Ru:**　①ル　　②レ　　③リ　　④ニ　　⑤ノ
17）**Wa:**①カ　　②ワ　　③ン　　④フ　　⑤ク
18）**Ka:**　①ラ　　②サ　　③ラ　　④チ　　⑤カ
19）**Ne:**　①ネ　　②ケ　　③ホ　　④チ　　⑤ロ
20）**To:**　①ユ　　②コ　　③ト　　④ロ　　⑤ニ

Practice 3: カタカナでかいてみよう。

Katakana is used for loanwords and foreign names. See the examples below.

①	**Lion**		r a i o n ライオン
②	**Koala**		ko a ra コアラ
③	**Virus**		u i ru su ウイルス
④	**Knife**		na i fu ナイフ
⑤	**Tire**		ta i ya タイヤ
⑥	**Ham**		ha mu ハム
⑦	**Towel**		ta o ru タオル
⑧	**Tie**		ne ku ta i ネクタイ

Listening and Speaking

Practice 1: おんせいをきいて、たんごをえらぼう。📢
Listen to the audio and choose the correct word.

1)	①レタス	②タコス	③タスク	④スイス
2)	①コント	②ロスト	③トマト	④アウト
3)	①マロン	②メロン	③サロン	④ナイロン
4)	①ワイン	②インコ	③ワニ	④コンロ
5)	①コメント	②コロコロ	③サイコロ	④アルカリ
6)	①テニス	②テント	③テスト	④アイス
7)	①ランチ	②ナイス	③ライス	④クラス
8)	①タスク	②リスク	③リスト	④コスト
9)	①アイス	②アニメ	③ロシア	④スイス
10)	①タイル	②タイム	③トイレ	④コイル

Practice 2: たんごをききとって、かいてみよう。📢
Listen to the audio and write down what you hear in the box.

①	Online						

②	Photographer						

③	Tunnel						

④	Handkerchief						

(5) Christmas

(6) Marathon

(7) Kiss

(8) United States (America)

(9) Recycle

(10) Restaurant

たんごリスト： **List of Japanese Vocabulary**

This is all the vocabulary you have learned in this lesson:

ライオン： lion

コアラ： koala

ウイルス： virus

ナイフ： knife

タイヤ： tire

ハム： ham

タオル： towel

ネクタイ： tie

レタス： lettuce

トマト： tomato

メロン： melon

ワイン： wine

コメント： comment

テスト： test

クラス： class

リスク： risk

アニメ： anime

トイレ： toilet

オンライン： online

カメラマン： cameraman

トンネル： tunnel

ハンカチ： handkerchief

クリスマス： Christmas

マラソン： marathon

キス： kiss

アメリカ： America

リサイクル： recycle

レストラン： restaurant

第5章
だい　　しょう

LESSON 5

カタカナの<ruby>濁点<rt>だくてん</rt></ruby>と<ruby>半濁点<rt>はんだくてん</rt></ruby>

Katakana with Diacritical Marks

もくひょう　Objective

- ✔ Learn how to read and write additional Japanese sounds using diacritical marks.
- ✔ Learn how to write the names of common items and the names of countries in katakana.

まなぶこと　Lesson Overview

Part 1: Katakana with Diacritical Marks (chart)

Part 2: Practice

Reading and Writing	**Listening and Speaking**
Practice 1	Practice 1
Practice 2	

Part 3: Country Name

Part 4: Where are you from?
Practice 1
Practice 2
Practice 3

List of Japanese Vocabulary

Part 1: Katakana with Diacritical Marks

In the chart below, you will see all 25 katakana characters with diacritical marks and the corresponding letters of the alphabet. Pay careful attention to the pronunciation of each character. Listen to the audio and repeat. 📢

ガ	ギ	グ	ゲ	ゴ
ga	gi	gu	ge	go
ザ	ジ	ズ	ゼ	ゾ
za	ji	zu	ze	zo
ダ	ヂ	ヅ	デ	ド
da	ji*1	zu*2	de	do
バ	ビ	ブ	ベ	ボ
ba	bi	bu	be	bo
パ	ピ	プ	ペ	ポ
pa	pi	pu	pe	po

*1ジ (ji) and ヂ (ji) sound the same. *2ズ (zu) and ヅ (zu) sound the same.

Just like the hiragana with a *dakuten* (゛), the consonants *k, s, t* and *h* become the consonants *g, z, d, b,* respectively. The sound of voiced consonants is stronger and comes from the throat and this should be accompanied by a puff of air as you pronounce it. The consonant *h* changes to a *p* sound with a *handakuten* (゜).

Part 2: れんしゅう Practice

Reading and Writing

As you write katakana with *dakuten* and *handakuten*, read them aloud. Pay close attention to the stroke order and trace the light gray characters in the first box. Then practice writing them without the guide in the blank boxes.

Practice 1: れんしゅうしよう。

Practice writing katakana with diacritical marks.

① ガ(ga)

② ギ(gi)

③ グ(gu)

④ ゲ(ge)

⑤ ゴ(go)

1) **ga** so ri n / gasoline

2) **go** ri ra / gorilla

3) **ga** mu / gum

4) sa n **gu** ra su / sunglasses

5) **ge** su to / guest

6) **ga** ra su / glass

⑥ ザ (za)

ザ						

⑦ ジ (ji)

ジ						

⑧ ズ (zu)

ズ						

⑨ ゼ (ze)

ゼ						

⑩ ゾ (zo)

ゾ						

1) pi **za** / pizza

2) su ta **ji** o / studio

3) ra **ji** o / radio

4) ku i **zu** / quiz

5) sa i **zu** / size

6) a ma **zo** n / Amazon

⑪ ダ(da)

⑫ ヂ(ji)

⑬ ヅ(zu)

⑭ デ(de)

⑮ ド(do)

1) **da** n su / dance

2) **de** za i n / design

3) mo **de** ru / model

4) gu ra u n **do** / sports field

5) **do** a / door

6) **do** ra ma / drama

⑯ バ(ba)

⑰ ビ(bi)

⑱ ブ(bu)

⑲ ベ(be)

⑳ ボ(bo)

1) **ba** ra n su / balance

2) **bi** ta mi n / vitamin

3) te re **bi** / TV

4) **bu** ra n do / brand

5) zu **bo** n / pants

6) **be** te ra n / expert

㉑ パ(pa)

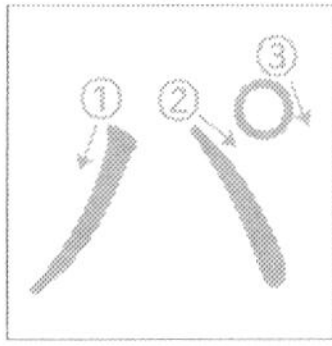

㉒ ピ(pi)

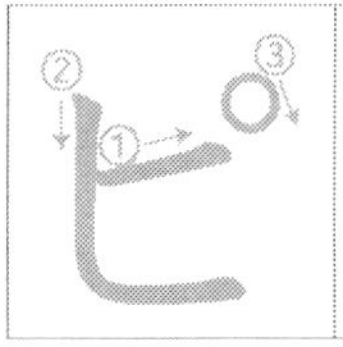

㉓ プ(pu)

㉔ ペ(pe)

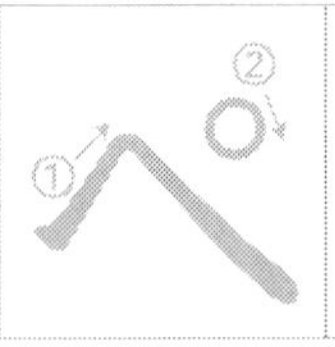

㉕ ポ(po)

1) **pa** n / bread

2) **pa** so ko n / PC

3) **pi** a no / piano

4) **pu** ro gu ra mu / program

5) **pe** n gi n / penguin

6) **po** i n to / point

Practice 2: ただしいカタカナをえらぼう。

Choose the correct katakana character.

1) Gu: ①ダ ②ガ ③べ ④ブ ⑤グ

2) Ji: ①グ ②ジ ③バ ④べ ⑤ペ

3) De: ①テ ②ゲ ③ポ ④デ ⑤バ

4) Bo: ①ボ ②ポ ③ド ④ザ ⑤ガ

5) Pa: ①バ ②パ ③ピ ④ペ ⑤プ

6) Ga: ①カ ②ゴ ③ガ ④グ ⑤ピ

7) Zo: ①ゼ ②セ ③ゾ ④ボ ⑤ギ

8) Do: ①ヂ ②ヅ ③ポ ④ボ ⑤ド

9) Pi: ①ピ ②プ ③ギ ④ペ ⑤ザ

10) Go: ①ロ ②ゴ ③グ ④べ ⑤ペ

Listening and Speaking

Practice 1: たんごをききとって、かいてみよう。📢

Listen to the audio and write down what you hear in the box.

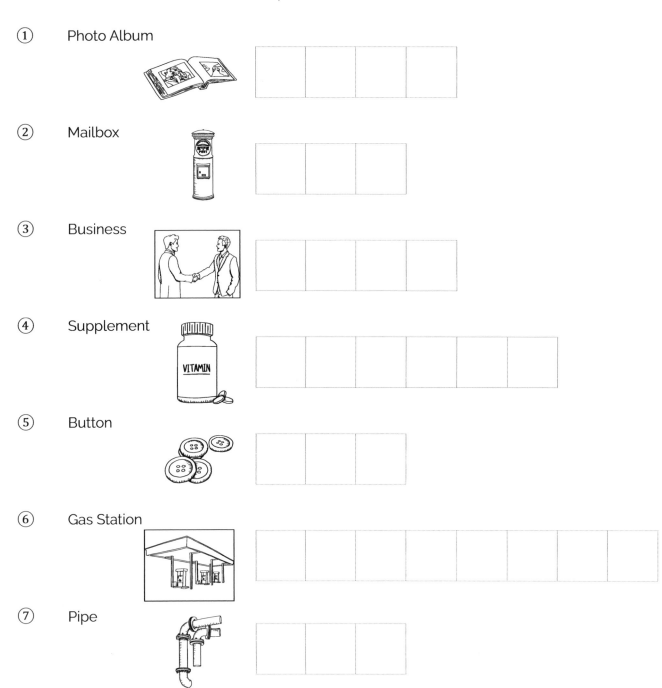

① Photo Album

② Mailbox

③ Business

④ Supplement

⑤ Button

⑥ Gas Station

⑦ Pipe

⑧　Engineer

　　　□ □ □ □ □

⑨　Part-time Job

　　　□ □ □ □ □

⑩　Visa

　　　□ □

⑪　Diamond

　　　□ □ □ □ □ □

⑫　Iguana

　　　□ □ □ □

⑬　Rhinoceros beetle

　　　□ □ □ □ □

⑭　Panda

　　　□ □

⑮　Crawfish

　　　□ □ □ □

Part 3: 国のなまえ Country Names

くに

The majority of country names are written in katakana. Below you will see a world map and a list of countries. Some of the country names from the world map are listed. Listen to the audio and pronounce each name aloud, then trace the light gray characters in the box. 📢

Asia アジア			⑩ Australia**	オーストラリア
① Japan*	日本	にほん	⑪ New Zealand**	ニュージーランド
② China*	中国	ちゅうごく	⑫ India	インド
③ Korea*	韓国	かんこく	**Middle East** 中東　ちゅうとう	
④ Mongolia	モンゴル		⑬ Pakistan	パキスタン
⑤ Vietnam	ベトナム		⑭ Iran	イラン
⑥ Thailand	タイ		⑮ Saudi Arabia	サウジアラビア
⑦ Philippines**	フィリピン		⑯ Israel	イスラエル
⑧ Malaysia**	マレーシア		⑰ Egypt	エジプト
⑨ Indonesia	インドネシア		⑱ Turkey	トルコ

Europe ヨーロッパ			㉜ Ghana**	ガーナ
⑲ Russia	ロシア		㉝ Liberia	リベリア
⑳ Ukraine	ウクライナ		㉞ South Africa***	南アフリカ
㉑ Poland**	ポーランド		**North and South America** 北アメリカ、南アメリカ	
㉒ Germany	ドイツ		㉟ Canada	カナダ
㉓ France	フランス		㊱ America (U.S.)	アメリカ
㉔ Italy	イタリア		㊲ Mexico	メキシコ
㉕ Spain	スペイン		㊳ Panama	パナマ
㉖ Portugal	ポルトガル		㊴ Colombia	コロンビア
㉗ United Kingdom	イギリス		㊵ Venezuela	ベネズエラ
Africa アフリカ			㊶ Peru**	ペルー
㉘ Kenya	ケニア		㊷ Bolivia	ボリビア
㉙ Ethiopia	エチオピア		㊸ Paraguay	パラグアイ
㉚ Uganda	ウガンダ		㊹ Argentina	アルゼンチン
㉛ Nigeria	ナイジェリア		㊺ Brazil	ブラジル

* These country names are commonly written in kanji.

** These country names contain the contracted sound and long vowel. You will learn more about it in Lesson 6.

*** This country's name contains a kanji character. The word "south" is commonly written in kanji but not in hiragana or katakana.

Part 4: 出身はどこですか？ Where are you from?

しゅっしん (furigana above 出身)

Imagine yourself traveling around in Japan. One of the first questions that a native would ask you, besides your name, would be your nationality. In this lesson, you will learn how to ask and respond to the common question "Where are you from?" There are number of ways to ask the question "Where are you from?" in Japanese. See the examples below. Listen to the audio and repeat each phrase. 📢

1. しゅっしんはどこですか？
The direct translation of this phrase is "What is your origin?"

This is a polite way to ask "Where are you from?" in Japanese. The Japanese word *shusshin* (出身) means your origin. In this case, your answer can be the name of the city or country where you were born or raised.

2. どこからきたんですか？
This phrase literally means "Where did you come from?" This is also polite enough to ask a stranger. Now let's practice how to answer the question, "Where are you from?" Add the name of any country or city in the box below to answer the question.

1. ☐ です。 I am from....

2. ☐ からきました。 I came from....

In Japanese, nationalities and ethnicities usually end with the character "人 (jin)". For example, アメリカ (America/United States) is the name of the country, but アメリカ人 means American. Maybe you have lived in a foreign country for many years and your nationality is from a different country. If you want to explain your ethnicity or nationality, you can use phrase #3.

3. わたしは ☐ 人 です。 I am.....

Practice 1: じぶんの国の名前を日本語で書いてみよう。

In the box below, write the name of your country in Japanese and complete the sentence.

[   ]です。 　I'm from (the name of your country or city)

[   ]からきました。 　I came from (the name of your country or city)

わたしは [   ]人 です。 　I am (your nationality or ethnicity)

Practice 2: 3人の会話をよんで、それぞれの出身を答えよう。

Below is a conversation between three people using the new phrases we have just learned in Part 4.
Read the conversation, then provide answers for where Hiroko, Sarah, and Noa are from.

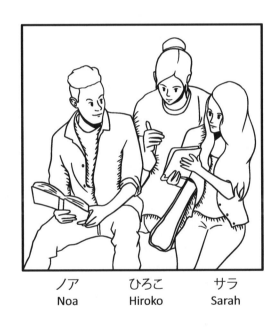

ノア　　ひろこ　　サラ
Noa　　Hiroko　　Sarah

ひろこ：こんにちは、サラさん。出身はどこです
か？

サラ：こんにちは、ひろこさん。イギリスからき
ました。ひろこさんは、どこからきたんですか？

ひろこ：わたしは日本からきました。

サラ：すごい！

ひろこ：ノアさん、はじめまして。どこからきた
んですか？

ノア：わたしは南 アフリカ人 です。

Name	Origin
Hiroko	
Sarah	
Noa	

Practice 3: 音声をきいて、どこの国の人かききとろう。

Meet some students from all over the world. Listen to the audio and write the names of the countries you hear in the box below. 📣

①ソア　②サンディ　③アラダ　④リサ　⑤シンジ　⑥ネルソン　⑦フアン　⑧トム

①	Q:出身はどこですか?	ソア:
②	Q:どこからきたんですか?	サンディ:
③	Q:出身はどこですか?	アラダ:
④	Q:どこからきたんですか?	リサ:
⑤	Q:出身はどこですか?	シンジ:
⑥	Q:どこからきたんですか?	ネルソン:
⑦	Q:出身はどこですか?	フアン:
⑧	Q:どこからきたんですか?	トム:

単語リスト：List of Japanese Vocabulary
たんご

This is all the vocabulary you have learned in this lesson:

ガソリン：gasoline
ゴリラ：gorilla
ガム：gum
サングラス：sunglasses
ゲスト：guest
ガラス：glass
ピザ：pizza
スタジオ：studio
ラジオ：radio
クイズ：quiz
サイズ：size
アマゾン：Amazon
ダンス：dance
デザイン：design
モデル：model
グラウンド：ground/field
ドア：door
ドラマ：drama
バランス：balance
ビタミン：vitamin
テレビ：TV
ブランド：brand
ズボン：pants

ベテラン：expert
パン：bread
パソコン：PC
ピアノ：piano
プログラム：program
ペンギン：penguin
ポイント：point
アルバム：photo album
ポスト：mailbox
ビジネス：business
サプリメント：supplement
ボタン：button
ガソリンスタンド：gas station
パイプ：pipe
エンジニア：engineer
アルバイト：part-time job
ビザ：visa
ダイヤモンド：diamond
イグアナ：iguana
カブトムシ：rhinoceros beetle
パンダ：panda
ザリガニ：crawfish

だい しょう
第6章
LESSON 6

カタカナの拗音、促音、特殊音、長音

<ruby>拗音<rt>ようおん</rt></ruby> <ruby>促音<rt>そくおん</rt></ruby> <ruby>特殊音<rt>とくしゅおん</rt></ruby> <ruby>長音<rt>ちょうおん</rt></ruby>

Contracted Sounds, Double Consonants, Special Sounds and Long Vowels in Katakana

もくひょう Objective

- Learn how to read and write contracted sounds, double consonants, special sounds and long vowels.
- ⬜Learn how to write the names of different foods, electronics and sports.
- ⬜Learn how to ask the question "What is…?" and how to express what you like.

まなぶこと Lesson Overview

Part 1: Contracted Sounds, Double Consonants, Special Sounds and Long Vowels.

1) Contracted Sounds (Small ヤ、ユ、ヨ)   3) Special Sounds in katakana
2) Double Consonants (Small ツ)   4) Long Vowels

Part 2: Practice

Reading and Writing   **Listening and Speaking**
Practice 1   Practice 1
Practice 2   Practice 2
Practice 3

Part 3: Vocabulary

Part 4: How to Order Food in a Restaurant

Part 5: What is This?

Part 6: Things That You Like and Things That You Don't Like.

List of Japanese Vocabulary

Part 1: Contracted Sounds, Double Consonants, Special Sounds and Long Vowels

1) Contracted Sounds 📢

Listen to the audio and repeat. Pay careful attention to the pronunciation of each character.

キャ	キュ	キョ	ギャ	ギュ	ギョ
kya	kyu	kyo	gya	gyu	gyo
シャ	シュ	ショ	ジャ	ジュ	ジョ
sha	shu	sho	ja	ju	jo
チャ	チュ	チョ			
cha	chu	cho			
ニャ	ニュ	ニョ			
nya	nyu	nyo			
ヒャ	ヒュ	ヒョ	ビャ	ビュ	ビョ
hya	hyu	hyo	bya	byu	byo
ミャ	ミュ	ミョ	ピャ	ピュ	ピョ
mya	myu	myo	pya	pyu	pyo
リャ	リュ	リョ			
rya	ryu	ryo			

2) Double Consonants (Small "tsu") 📢

The small letter ツ is used when transcribing double consonants such as *tt* and *pp*. Look at the examples below. Listen carefully to the audio and repeat.

カップ (kappu) cup
バッグ (baggu) bag
キック(kikku) kick

ロック (rokku) rock
セット (setto) set
ペット (petto) pet

3) Special Sounds 📢

Over time, as more and more foreign words made their way into Japanese, people realized that the existing katakana did not provide an accurate enough representation for some sounds. For example, the letter "V" in English has no equivalent in the Japanese sound system. So, in 1991, the Japanese government officially created a list of new katakana combinations as a guideline for more accurately representing the original sounds of the foreign languages. Here they are below.

The katakana characters in Chart 1 are most commonly used for transliterating foreign names, whereas the ones in Chart 2 are only used in very uncommon words.

Chart 1

			シェ	
			she	
			チェ	
			che	
ツァ			ツェ	ツォ
tsa			tse	tso
	ティ			
	ti			
ファ	フィ		フェ	フォ
fa	fi		fe	fo
			ジェ	
			je	
	ディ			
	di			
		デュ		
		dyu		

Chart 2

			イェ	
			ye	
	ウィ		ウェ	ウォ
	wi		we	wo
クァ	クィ		クェ	クォ
kwa	kwi		kwe	kwo
	ツィ			
	tsi			
		トゥ		
		tu		
グァ				
gwa				
		ドゥ		
		du		
ヴァ	ヴィ	ヴ	ヴェ	ヴォ
va	vi	vu	ve	vo
		テュ		
		tyu		
		フュ		
		fyu		
		ヴュ		
		vyu		

4) Long Vowels 📢

The long vowel sounds are written with a dash (—) called a *Chōon* (長音) mark in katakana. See the examples below.

ツアー (tsuaa) / tour　　　　　　スーツ (suutsu) ／ suit
ケーキ (ke-ki) / cake　　　　　　ボール (booru) / ball
スキー (sukii) ／ ski　　　　　　リゾート (rizooto) / resort

Part 2: れんしゅう Practice

Reading and Writing

As you write each katakana character with the small ヤ、ユ and ヨ, read it aloud. Pay close attention to the stroke order and trace the light gray characters in the first box. Then practice writing them without the guide in the blank boxes.

Practice 1: れんしゅうしよう。

Practice writing katakana with the small letters.

1) Kya

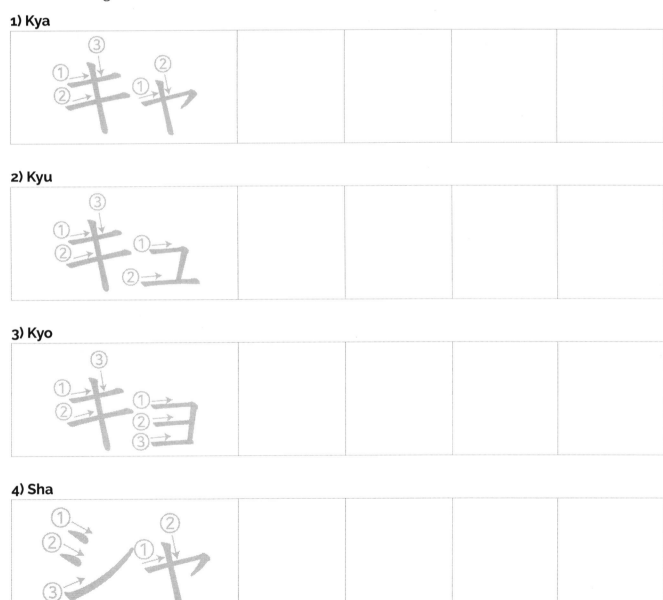

2) Kyu

3) Kyo

4) Sha

5) Shu

6) Sho

7) Cha

8) Chu

9) Cho

10) Nya

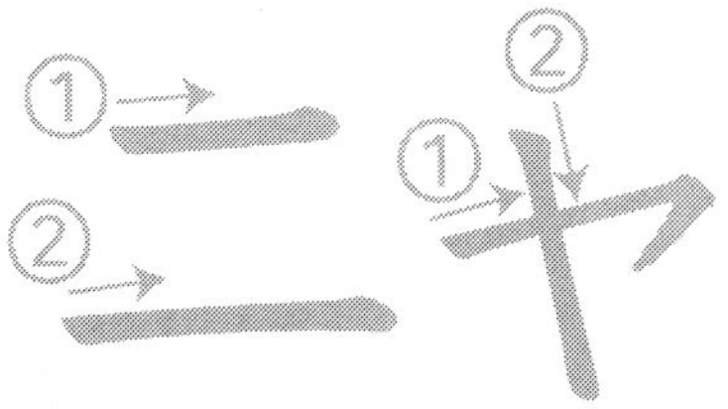

二ャ

11) Nyu

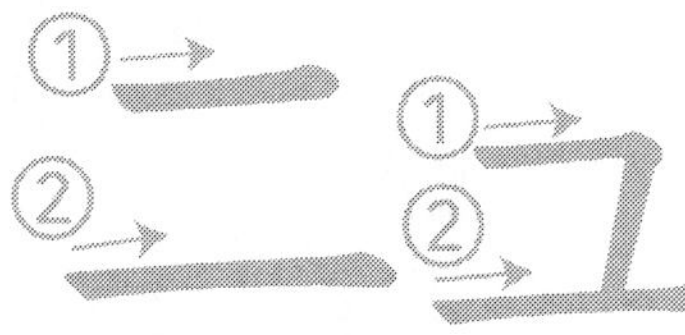

ニュ

12) Nyo

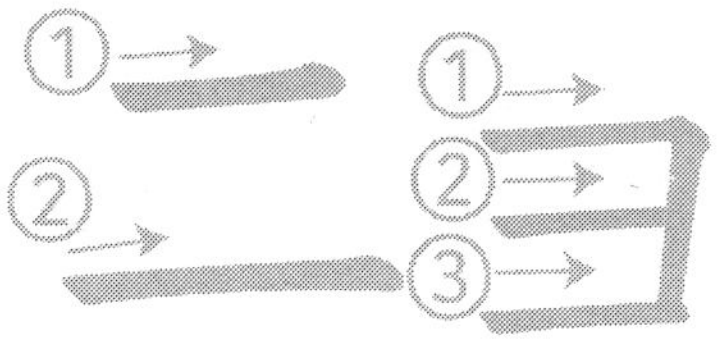

ニョ

13) Hya

ヒャ

14) Hyu

ヒュ

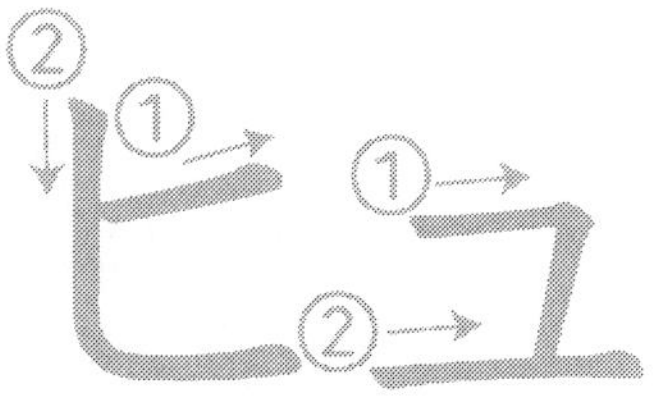

15) Hyo

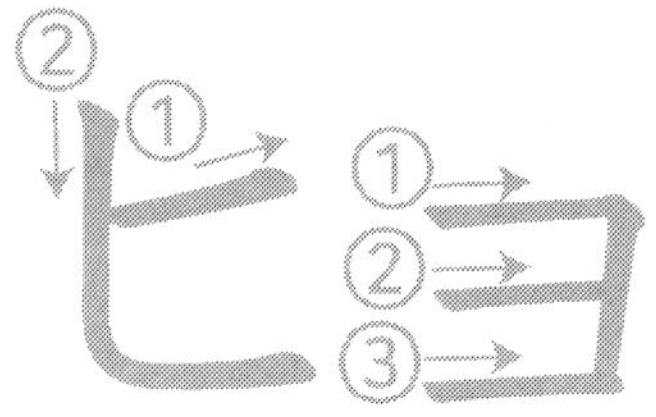

ヒョ

16) Mya

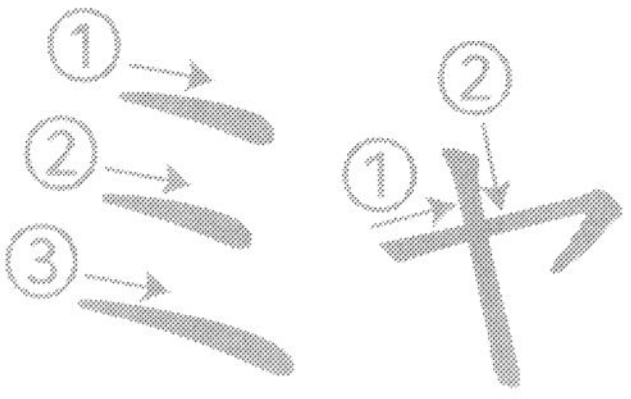

ミャ

17) Myu

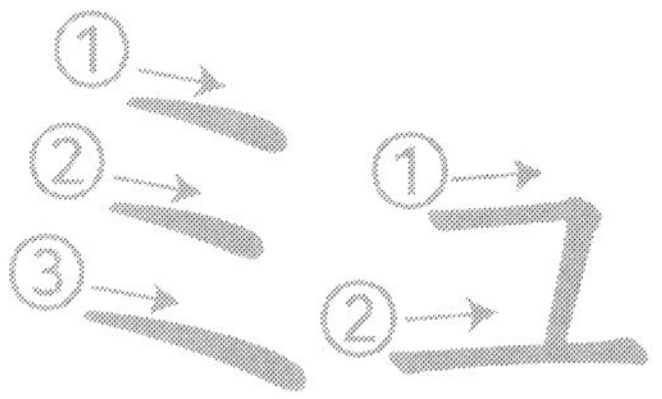

ミュ

18) Myo

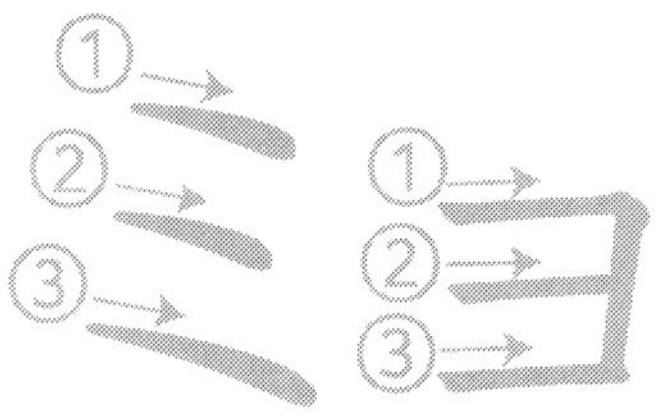

ミョ

19) Rya

リャ

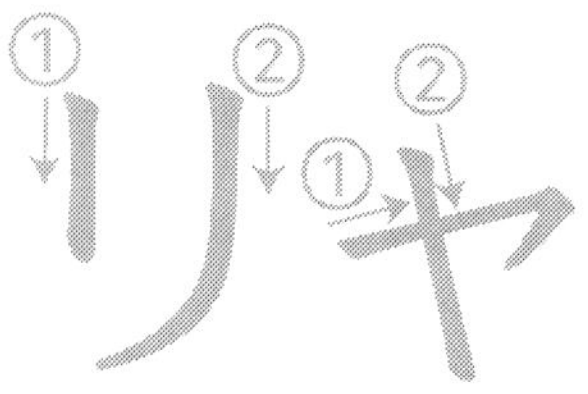

20) Ryu

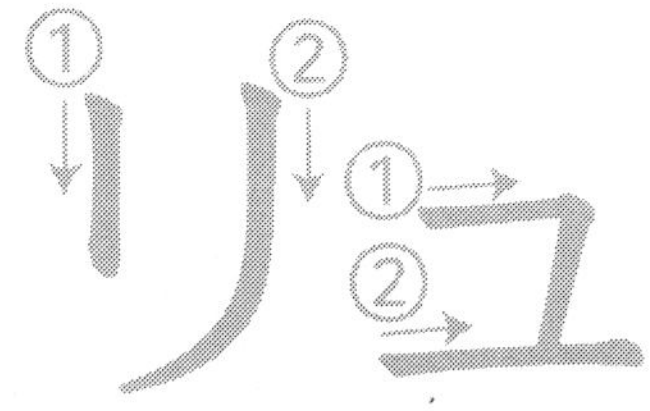

リュ

21) Ryo

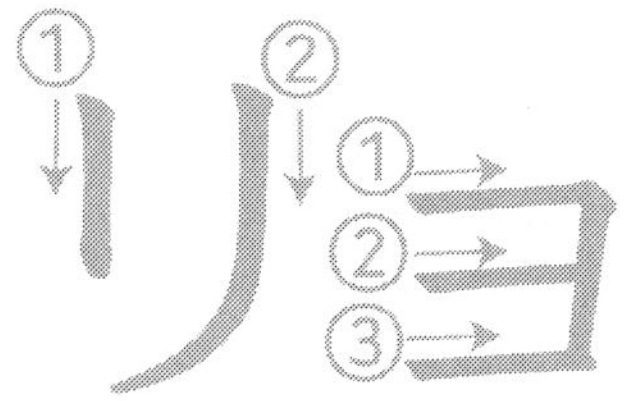

リョ

22) Gya

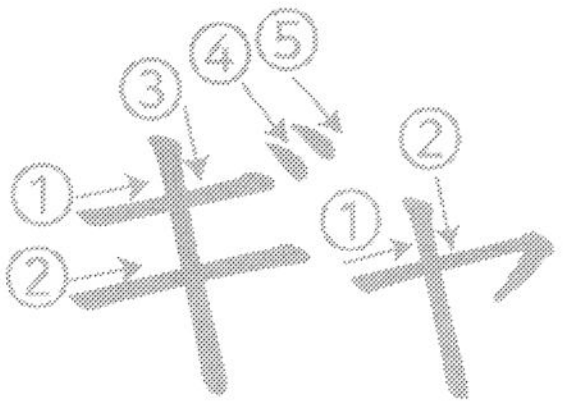

ギャ

23) Gyu

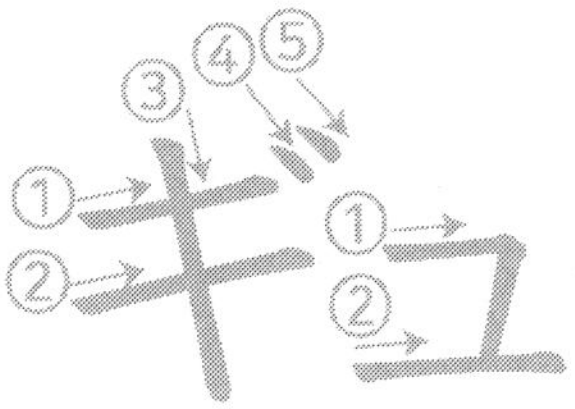

ギュ

24) Gyo

ギョ

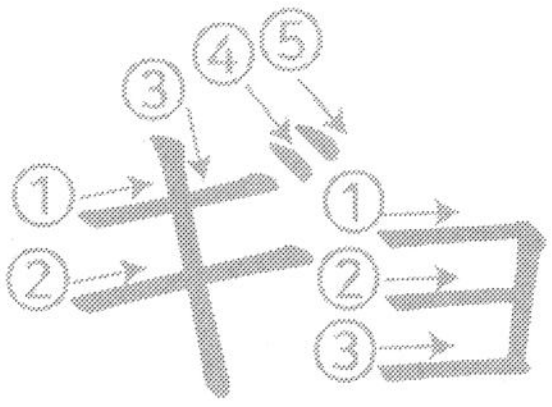

25) Ja

ジャ

26) Ju

ジュ

27) Jo

ジョ

28) Bya

ビャ

29) Byu

ビュ

30) Byo

31) Pya

32) Pyu

33) Pyo

Practice 2: ただしいカタカナをえらぼう。
Select the correct katakana character.

1) **Kyu:** ①キャ ②ギャ ③キュ ④シュ ⑤ニュ

2) **Sha:** ①シャ ②ジャ ③ギャ ④ビュ ⑤ビョ

3) **Nya:** ①チャ ②ニャ ③シャ ④チャ ⑤ピャ

4) **Hyo:** ①ジョ ②ビョ ③ヒョ ④キャ ⑤ピュ

5) **Mya:** ①キョ ②ギャ ③リャ ④ヒャ ⑤ミャ

6) **Rya:** ①チュ ②チャ ③リャ ④リョ ⑤ジョ

7) **Gyo:** ①ギョ ②ショ ③キョ ④ジャ ⑤ジュ

8) **Bya:** ①チョ ②チャ ③シャ ④ビュ ⑤ビャ

9) **Pyu:** ①ピュ ②ジュ ③キュ ④ピャ ⑤チョ

10) **Ju:** ①ジュ ②シュ ③ジャ ④ジュ ⑤リャ

11) **Kya:** ①リャ ②キャ ③ギャ ④キョ ⑤ショ

12) **Byo:** ①ジョ ②ビャ ③ギョ ④ビョ ⑤ヒョ

13) **Ryu:** ①リュ ②リョ ③キュ ④シュ ⑤リャ

14) **Di:** ①ヴィ ②ディ ③ティ ④クィ ⑤ツィ

15) **Fi:** ①ファ ②フェ ③ビャ ④フォ ⑤フィ

16) **Va:** ①グァ ②ヴィ ③ウィ ④ヴァ ⑤ヴォ

17) **Je:** ①シェ ②ジェ ③ジャ ④ジョ ⑤ヴュ

18) **Ye:** ①トゥ ②ウィ ③イェ ④ツェ ⑤クェ

Practice 3: カタカナをよんでみよう。

Read the words in katakana and then draw a line to match each word to the appropriate picture.

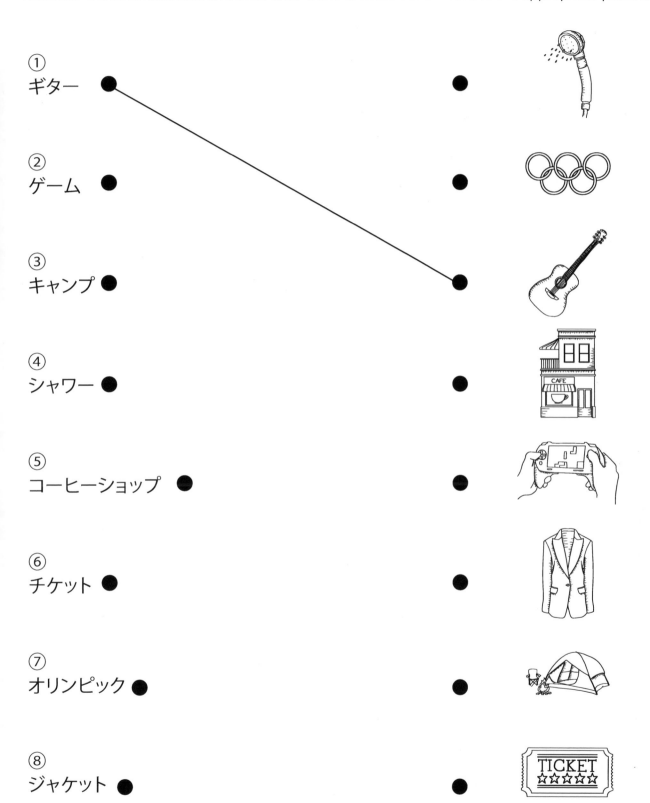

① ギター ●

② ゲーム ●

③ キャンプ ●

④ シャワー ●

⑤ コーヒーショップ ●

⑥ チケット ●

⑦ オリンピック ●

⑧ ジャケット ●

Listening and Speaking

Practice 1: 音声<ruby>おんせい</ruby>をきいて、単語<ruby>たんご</ruby>をえらぼう。📢

Listen to the audio and choose the correct word.

1.	①ジャム	②ジャズ	③シャツ	④チョーク
2.	①バリュー	②メニュー	③ジュース	④ニュース
3.	①アパート	②デパート	③スプーン	④ビニール
4.	①デート	②コーヒー	③データ	④セール
5.	①ギター	②ピアノ	③セーター	④ジーンズ

Practice 2: 単語<ruby>たんご</ruby>を聞<ruby>き</ruby>き取<ruby>と</ruby>って、書<ruby>か</ruby>いてみよう。📢

Listen to the audio and write down what you hear in the box.

① File

② Soup

③ Surfing

④ Sofa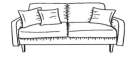

⑤ Table

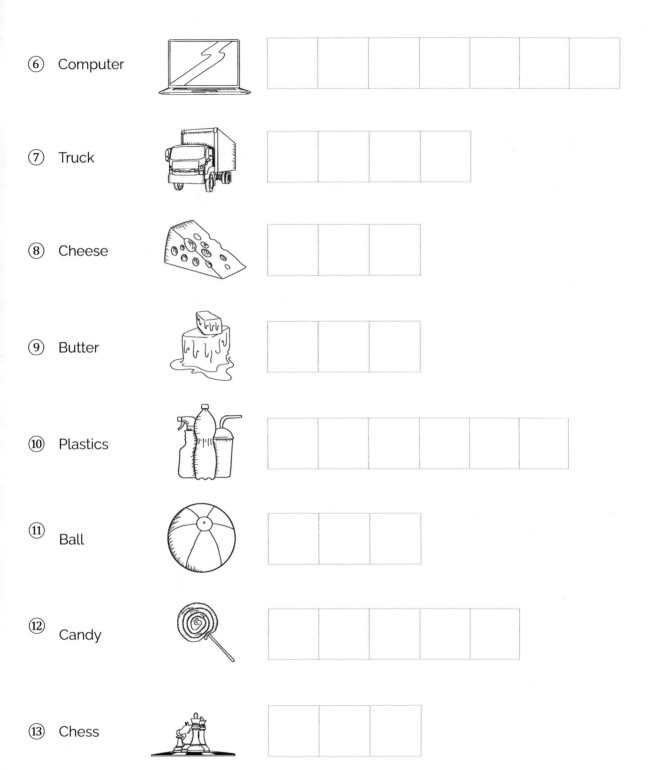

⑥ Computer

⑦ Truck

⑧ Cheese

⑨ Butter

⑩ Plastics

⑪ Ball

⑫ Candy

⑬ Chess

Part 3: Vocabulary

Practice 1: 電子機器の名前を覚えよう。

The names of many electronic devices are written in katakana.
Fill in the boxes below with the right name.

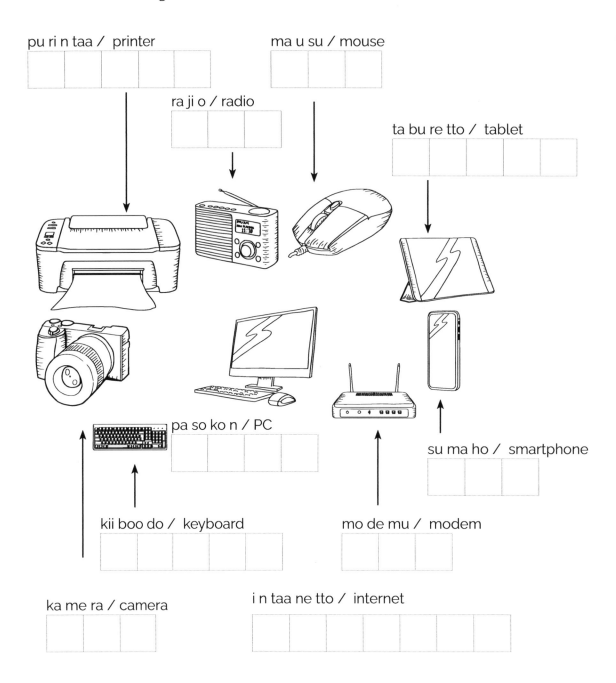

pu ri n taa / printer

ma u su / mouse

ra ji o / radio

ta bu re tto / tablet

pa so ko n / PC

su ma ho / smartphone

kii boo do / keyboard

mo de mu / modem

ka me ra / camera

i n taa ne tto / internet

Practice 2: スポーツの名前を覚えよう。

Many sports are written in katakana. Fill in the empty spaces below with the name of the sport corresponding to each number.

	Su poo tsu / Sport	⑤	Ba su ke tto boo ru / Basketball
	スポーツ		
①	Te ni su / Tennis	⑥	Sa kkaa / Soccer
②	A i su ho kkee / Ice hockey	⑦	Su kii / Skiing
③	Ya kyu u / Baseball *	⑧	Ra gu bii / Rugby
④	Va ree boo ru / Volleyball	⑨	Go ru fu / Golf

* Yakyuu (野球) is commonly written in kanji or hiragana as it is not a foreign word.

Part 4: 日本語<ruby>にほんご</ruby>で注文<ruby>ちゅうもん</ruby>してみよう。 How to order food in a restaurant

Imagine yourself in a restaurant in Japan. After the server has handed you the menu and given you some time to look it over, they usually ask "Gochumon wa okimari desuka?" which means "Are you ready to order?"

ごちゅうもんはおきまりですか？
Are you ready to order?

はい、ご注文はお決まりですか？

すみません！

To place your order, follow the sentence structure below. In the first box, say the name of the dish. Then add a number with a "counter" to indicate how many servings. In Japanese, there are words called "counters" that are combined with a number to specify the quantity of something. Different types of things, such as servings of food, people, books, and so on, all use different counters. You cannot only state the numbers you learned in Lesson 3 by themselves. You must use the number and the appropriate counter together. Refer to the words in the box below. It shows the counting system for most types of food.

Name of the dish	を	**Number**	おねがいします。

(Name of the dish) wo (Number) onegai shimasu. / Please give me ～.

General Food Counter

1	ひとつ hitotsu	4	よっつ yottsu
2	ふたつ futatsu	5	いつつ itsutsu
3	みっつ mittsu	6	むっつ muttsu

*You probably wouldn't order more than 5 dishes in a restaurant. But if you want to buy something else at a store, you can use another counter, "ko." This counter is used for small items such as tomatoes, apples and candy. Here is how to use the counter "ko" with the numbers 1 to 10. 1: いっこ; 2: にこ; 3: さんこ; 4: よんこ; 5: ごこ; 6: ろっこ; 7: ななこ; 8: はっこ; 9: きゅうこ; and 10: じゅっこ

Example: 📢

Here is a typical conversation at a restaurant. Listen to the conversation of a family at the restaurant and repeat.

Server: メニューをどうぞ。
Here is the menu.

Family: ありがとうございます。
Thank you very much.

Server: ごちゅうもんはおきまりですか？
Are you ready to order?

Family: はい。ラーメンをみっつおねがいします。
Yes. Three bowls of ramen, please.

Server: おのみものはどうしますか？
Would you like something to drink?

Family: はい。みずをみっつ、ビールをひとつおねがいします。
Yes. Three glasses of water and one bottle of beer, please.

Server: かしこまりました。
OK, coming right up!

Practice 1: メニューの食べ物の名前をカタカナで書いてみよう。

Usually, the names of foreign dishes on a menu are written in katakana. On the menu below, all the foreign foods are written in hiragana. In the boxes provided below the menu, rewrite the name of each food item in katakana.

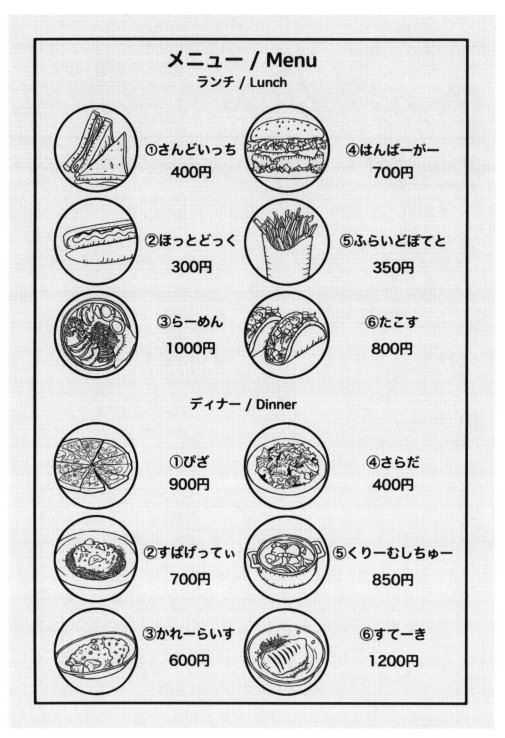

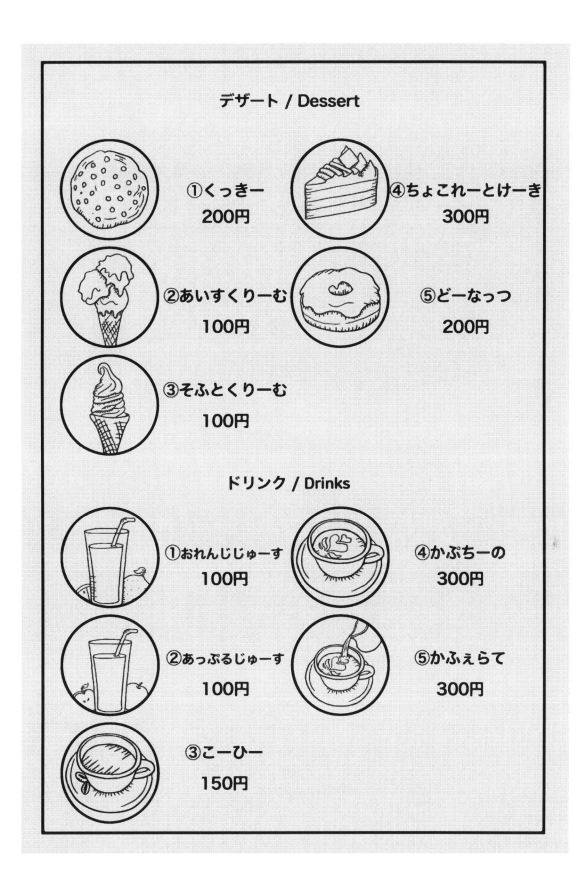

デザート / Dessert

①くっきー
200円

④ちょこれーとけーき
300円

②あいすくりーむ
100円

⑤どーなっつ
200円

③そふとくりーむ
100円

ドリンク / Drinks

①おれんじじゅーす
100円

④かぷちーの
300円

②あっぷるじゅーす
100円

⑤かふぇらて
300円

③こーひー
150円

	Lunch		
①		④	
②		⑤	
③		⑥	

	Dinner		
①		④	
②		⑤	
③		⑥	

	Dessert		
①		④	
②		⑤	
③			

	Drinks		
①		④	
②		⑤	
③			

Practice 2: 食べ物を注文するときの文章を書いてみよう。

Write a sentence to order each food in the corresponding box.

	Food	In Japanese
①	3 sandwiches	
②	2 ice creams	
③	1 apple Juice	
④	1 pizza, 1 hamburger	

Practice 3: 会話を聞いて、何を注文したのか聞き取ろう。📢

Shinji and Sandy are at the restaurant. They try to order some food. Listen to the audio carefully and answer the questions below.

シンジ：すいません。

ウエイター：はい。ごちゅうもんはおきまりですか？

シンジ：はい、＿＿＿①＿＿＿を＿＿＿①＿＿＿おねがいします。

サンディー：わたしは、＿＿＿②＿＿＿を＿＿＿②＿＿＿、＿＿＿②＿＿＿を＿②＿おねがいします。

ウエイター：おのみものはどうしますか？

シンジ：はい、＿＿＿①＿＿＿を＿＿＿①＿＿＿おねがいします。

サンディ：＿＿＿＿②＿＿＿を＿＿＿②＿＿＿おねがいします。

ウエイター：かしこまりました。

シンジ：いくらですか？

ウエイター：＿＿＿③＿＿＿えんです。

サンディ：ありがとうございます。

① What did Shinji order?

_____

② What did Sandy order?

_____

③ What is the total price?

_____

Part 5: これは何<ruby>何<rt>なん</rt></ruby>ですか？　What is this?

Now let's practice how to ask the question "What is this?" and listen to the answer. When you are looking at a menu in a restaurant or when you are at a store, if you find something interesting and you want to ask: "What is this?" in Japanese, point to the item and say "Kore wa nan desuka? (What is this?)". なに (nani) or なん (nan) means "what?" in Japanese.

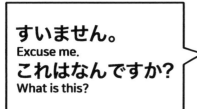

すいません。
Excuse me.
これはなんですか?
What is this?

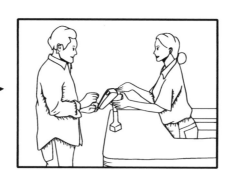

それは（　　　　　）です。
That is . . .

Practice 1: 音声<rt>おんせい</rt>を聞<rt>き</rt>いて、空白<rt>くうはく</rt>を埋<rt>う</rt>めよう。📢
Listen to the audio and fill in the blank spaces.

① At the electronics store
おきゃく：これはなんですか？
てんいん：それは（　　　　　　　　）です。

② At the electronics store
おきゃく：これはなんですか？
てんいん：それは（　　　　　　　　）です。

③ In a restaurant
おきゃく：これはなんですか？
てんいん：それは（　　　　　　　　）です。

④ In a restaurant
おきゃく：これはなんですか？
てんいん：それは（　　　　　　　　）です。

Part 6: 好<ruby>好<rt>す</rt></ruby>きなものを<ruby>説明<rt>せつめい</rt></ruby>しよう。 Explaining what you like

In this section, you will learn how to express your likes and dislikes in Japanese. Follow the grammar pattern below. If you are talking about what you like, you can add "わたし (watashi)"* which means "I" in the first box. If you are talking about somebody else, you can add the person's name or their title in the box. *It's often left out if it is obvious that you are the person who likes/dislikes the thing.

| The name of the person | は | Noun | がすきです。 |

(The name of the person) wa (Noun) ga suki desu. / 〜 like something.

| The name of the person | は | Noun | がすきじゃないです。 |

(Name of the person) wa (Noun) ga suki janai desu. / 〜 doesn't like something.

In the second box for nouns, you can add anything: a sport, a dish, an animal or a country. However, if you mention the name of a person, it is sometimes understood that you are romantically interested in that person. So be careful!

If you like something a lot, you can use だいすき (dai suki) instead of すき (suki) to intensify the feeling conveyed.

If you don't like something, you can use すきじゃない. But if you want to take it a step further and say you really hate something, use きらい (kirai) instead of すきじゃない (suki janai).

Read the example below aloud. Pay close attention to the sentence structure.

Example:

<u>わたし</u>は<u>スパゲッティ</u>がすきです。 *I like spaghetti.*
  I   food

<u>サンディ</u>は<u>ねこ</u>がすきです。 *Sandy likes cats.*
  name   animal

<u>リサ</u>は<u>テニス</u>がすきじゃないです。 *Lisa doesn't like tennis.*
name sport

Practice 1: 空白を埋めて、文を完成させよう。

Now think of the animals, foods, sports you like. Add the things you like in the spaces below and complete each sentence.

1. **Animal**

わたしは＿＿＿＿＿＿＿＿＿＿がすきです。

2. **Food**

わたしは＿＿＿＿＿＿＿＿＿＿がすきです。

3. **Sports**

わたしは＿＿＿＿＿＿＿＿＿＿がすきです。

Practice 2: 文を読んで問題に答えよう。

This is Tom from Lesson 5. Below are some of the things he likes and doesn't like. Read what he has to say and answer the questions that follow.

> わたしは日本がだいすきです。
> たべものでは、すしがだいすきです。
> でも、ラーメンはすきじゃないです。
> スポーツでは、バスケットボールがすきです。
> でも、サッカーはきらいです。

① What food does he like?

_____

② What sport does he like?

_____

③ What food does he not like?

_____

単語リスト：List of Japanese Vocabulary

たんご

This is all the vocabulary you have learned in this lesson:

カップ：cup
バック：bag
キック：kick
ロック：rock
セット：set
ペット：pet
ツアー：tour
ケーキ：cake
スキー：ski
スーツ：suit
ボール：ball
リゾート：resort
ギター：guitar
ゲーム：game
キャンプ：camp
シャワー：shower
コーヒーショップ：coffee shop, café
チケット：ticket
オリンピック：Olympics
ジャケット：jacket
シャツ：shirt
ニュース：news
ジーンズ：jeans
アパート：apartment
コーヒー：coffee
ファイル：file
スープ：soup
サーフィン：surfing
ソファー：sofa
テーブル：table
コンピューター：computer

トラック：truck
チーズ：cheese
バター：butter
プラスティック：plastics
ボール：ball
キャンディ：candy
チェス：chess
プリンター：printer
ラジオ：radio
マウス：mouse
タブレット：tablet
スマホ（スマートフォン）：smartphone
モデム：modem
インターネット：internet
キーボード：keyboard
カメラ：camera
パソコン：PC
テニス：tennis
アイスホッケー：ice hockey
やきゅう：baseball
バレー：volleyball
バスケットボール：basketball
サッカー：soccer
スキー：ski
ゴルフ：golf
ラグビー：rugby
ちゅうもん：order
のみもの：drink
ビール：beer
てんいん：shop staff, server
ウエイター：server

LESSON 7

自己紹介

Introduce Yourself in Japanese

もくひょう Objective

- ✔ Learn basic Japanese grammar rules to form sentences.
- ✔ ⊠Learn how to introduce yourself in Japanese.
- ✔ ⊠Learn how to explain what you are going to do in Japanese.

まなぶこと Lesson Overview

Part 1: Basic Japanese Grammar

Grammar 1: Noun$_1$ is/are Noun$_2$ Grammar 3: Adjectives

Grammar 2: Verbs   Grammar 4: Particles

Part 2: Practice

Reading and Writing

Listening and Speaking

Part 3: Introduce yourself in Japanese

Practice 1

Practice 2

Practice 3

Part 1: Basic Japanese Grammar

Japanese grammar patterns are quite different from English. In this section, you will learn the basic grammar you need to know before forming sentences in Japanese.

Grammar 1: Noun₁ is/are Noun₂

"I am John." "Mike is a student." "This is my school." These sentences, which do not contain verbs in Japanese, can be formed by using this grammar pattern.

$$\text{Noun}_1 \text{は Noun}_2 \text{です。} \quad \text{Noun}_1 + \text{is/are} + \text{Noun}_2.$$

For example:

わたしはジョンです。

I am John.

マイクはがくせいです。

Mike is a student.

これはわたしのがっこうです。

This is my school.

In Japanese, there is no word that corresponds to the article "a" or the plural "s" at the end of a noun. Pronouns can be omitted if it is clear from the context.

The term わたし (*watashi*) or ぼく (*boku*) is used to refer to yourself. While *watashi* is a genderless personal pronoun that can be used in business settings, *boku* sounds more casual and is often used by men. In Japanese, the second person pronoun "you" is *anata*. The third person pronoun "he" is *kare* and the pronoun "she" is *kanojo*. However, Japanese native speakers don't use these personal pronouns too often. Rather than using these personal pronouns, native speakers prefer using their own names in the conversation.

わたし	I (both men and women)
ぼく	I (only for men)
あなた*	You
かれ*	He
かのじょ*	She

*These personal pronouns are not used often.

Grammar 2: Verbs

"I will go to the library." "I study Japanese." "I play basketball." In this section, you will learn how to form sentences that contain verbs.

In Japanese the sentence order is quite different from English. See the example below.

Sentence Order: Subject + Object + Verb

わたしはバスケットボールをします。

I play basketball.

In English the basic sentence order is the Subject + Verb + Object. In Japanese the sentence order is the Subject + Object + Verb. A good rule to remember in Japanese is that the verb always goes at the end.

Below you will find a chart of some common verbs. It also illustrates how to conjugate each verb in the affirmative form and negative form. Take note that the affirmative and negative form of the verbs listed can either be used in the present tense or future tense.

	Plain Form	Affirmative	Negative
①	たべる **to eat**	たべる / たべます	たべない / たべません
	おきる **to get up**	おきる / おきます	おきない / おきません
	ねる **to go to bed**	ねる / ねます	ねない / ねません
	みる **to watch, to see**	みる / みます	みない / みません
	おしえる **to teach**	おしえる / おしえます	おしえない/ おしえません
②	いく **to go**	いく / いきます	いかない / いきません
	かえる **to go home**	かえる / かえります	かえらない / かえりません
	きく **to listen**	きく / ききます	きかない / ききません
	のむ **to drink**	のむ / のみます	のまない / のみません
	はなす **to speak**	はなす / はなします	はなさない / はなしません
	よむ **to read**	よむ / よみます	よまない / よみません
	はたらく **to work**	はたらく / はたらきます	はたらかない / はたらきません
③	べんきょうする **to study**	べんきょうする / べんきょうします	べんきょうしない / べんきょうしません
	する **to do, to play (sport)**	する / します	しない / しません
	くる **to come**	くる / きます	こない / きません

As you noticed in the list, there are three kinds of verbs in Japanese. The first group of verbs is called *ru*-verbs. The second group is called *u*-verbs. The third group is called irregular verbs. It is good to know what group each verb belongs to since each group is conjugated differently.

Below are some examples of how to conjugate each group of verbs.

Group 1: *ru*-verbs

The *ru*-verbs always start with the verb base and end with the suffix *ru*. The example below illustrates how to conjugate *ru*-verbs.

Plain Form	Affirmative	Negative
たべる	たべる / たべます	たべない / たべません
taberu	**taberu / tabemasu**	**tabenai / tabemasen**

Group 2: *u*-verbs

The second group of verbs is called *u*-verbs. The *u*-verbs start with the verb base and end with the suffix *u*. The example below illustrates how to conjugate *u*-verbs.

Plain Form	Affirmative	Negative
いく	いく / いきます	いかない / いきません
iku	**iku / ikimasu**	**ikanai / ikimasen**

Exceptions: Be careful because some *u*-verbs look like *ru*-verbs, for example かえる(kaeru), however this word falls into the second group.

Group3: Irregular verbs

There are two irregular verbs in Japanese, する (suru) and くる (kuru). These are the only two verbs that do not follow the conjugation patterns in group 1 or group 2 as discussed above.

Plain Form	Affirmative	Negative
する	する / します	しない / しません
suru	**suru / shimasu**	**shinai / shimasen**
くる	くる / きます	こない / きません
kuru	**kuru / kimasu**	**konai / kimasen**

Grammar 3: Adjectives

There are two groups of adjectives in Japanese. One group is called い-adjective and the other group is called な-adjective. These two groups of adjectives follow different conjugation patterns. Unlike in English, in Japanese you also need to conjugate adjectives depending on the tense, whether it be present or past tense.

	Plain form		Affirmative	Negative
い	あつい	*hot*	あつい	あつくない
	さむい	*cold*	さむい	さむくない
	おもしろい	*interesting, funny*	おもしろい	おもしろくない
	いそがしい	*busy*	いそがしい	いそがしくない
	たかい	*expensive*	たかい	たかくない
	やすい	*cheap*	やすい	やすくない
	おいしい	*tasty*	おいしい	おいしくない
	むずかしい	*difficult*	むずかしい	むずかしくない
な	げんきな	*healthy*	げんき	げんきじゃない
	しずかな	*quiet*	しずか	しずかじゃない
	きれいな	*beautiful*	きれい	きれいじゃない
	すきな	*favorite, to like*	すき	すきじゃない
	かんたんな	*easy*	かんたん	かんたんじゃない

"です (desu)" is an auxiliary verb and you can add it after these adjectives (affirmative and negative) to make it polite.

Group 1: い-adjective

All adjectives in this group end with い. See the example below to see the conjugation.

たかい	たかい（です）	たかくない（です）
takai	takai desu	takakunai desu

Example: ц

Plain form of adjective + noun: たかいふく   expensive clothing

Affirmative: このふくはたかい（です）。   This clothing is expensive.

Negative: このふくはたかくない（です）。   This clothing is not expensive.

Group 2 な-adjective

All adjectives in this group end with な. See the example below to see the conjugation.

きれいな	きれい（です）	きれいじゃない（です）
kireina	**kirei desu**	**kirei janai desu**

Example:

Plain form of adjective + noun: <u>きれいな</u><u>こうえん</u>　<u>Beautiful</u> <u>park</u>

Affirmative: <u>このこうえん</u><u>は</u><u>きれい</u>（です）。<u>This park</u> is <u>beautiful</u>.

Negative: <u>あのこうえん</u><u>は</u><u>きれいじゃない</u>（です）。<u>That park</u> is <u>not beautiful</u>.

Grammar 4: Particles

In this section, you will learn 6 particles and how each particle is used in a sentence.

は：Topic particle

This particle is written in hiragana は (ha). When it is used as a particle it is pronounced "wa." It comes after the topic of a sentence. It can be translated as "as for" or "speaking of" in English. See the examples below.

Example:

わたし<u>は</u>がっこうにいきます。　I am going to school.

きょう<u>は</u>あめです。As for today, it's rainy.

を：Object particle

The object particle usually comes after the direct object of an action. See the examples below.

Example:

えいが<u>を</u>みます。　I am going to watch a movie.

おちゃ<u>を</u>のみます。　I drink tea.

で：Location and method particle

The particle で indicates location. It can be translated as "in" or "at" in English. This particle is also used to indicate means. It can be translated as "by" or "with" in English.

Example:

いえ<u>で</u>えいがをみます。　I am going to watch a movie <u>at home</u>. (location)

くるま<u>で</u>シカゴにいきます。　I go to Chicago <u>by car</u>. (means)

に：**Goal of movement and time**

This particle is mainly used to indicate location, time or movement.

Example:

わたしはおおさか<u>に</u>すんでいます。I live <u>in Osaka</u>. (Location)

あしたがっこう<u>に</u>いきます。　I'm going <u>to school</u> tomorrow. (Goal of movement)

にちようび<u>に</u>えいがをみます。　I'm going to watch a movie <u>on Sunday</u>. (Time)

へ：**Goal of movement**

The particle へ also indicate the goal of movement. When it is used as a particle, it is pronounced as "e."

Example:

あしたがっこう<u>へ</u>いきます。　I'm going <u>to school</u> tomorrow. (Goal of movement)

の：**Possession**

The particle の connects two nouns. One of the main ways to use this particle is to indicate possession. It acts like the possessive "s" or "of" in English.

Example:

わたし<u>の</u>スマホ　my smartphone

わたし<u>の</u>おかあさん<u>の</u>ほん　My mother's book

わたし	I	わたしの〜	My〜
おおく	I	ぼくの〜	My〜
あなた	You	あなたの〜	Your〜
おかあさん	Mother	おかあさんの〜	My mother's〜
ジョン	John	ジョンの〜	John's〜

Part 2: れんしゅう Practice

Reading and Writing

Practice 1: 日本語を読んで正しいか、間違っているか答えよう。

Read the schedule below and state if the sentence is true or false.

Day	What to do
げつようび	ぎんこうへいきます。
かようび	にほんごをべんきょうします。
すいようび	ほんをよみます。
もくようび	としょかんにいきます。
きんようび	えいがをみます。
どようび	すしをたべます。
にちようび	バスケットボールをします。

① He studies English on Tuesday.　（True/False）

② He reads a book on Wednesday.　（True/False）

③ He watches a movie on Friday.　（True/False）

④ He eats Sushi on Thursday.　（True/False）

⑤ He plays basketball on Sunday.　（True/False）

Practice 2: 空白にはいる言葉をえらぼう。

Choose an appropriate particle to fill in the blank spaces.

① がっこう____いきます。 I'm going to the school.

1. は　　　　2. に　　3. を　　4. の　　5. で

② サッカー____します。 I play soccer.

1. は　　　　2. に　　3. を　　4. の　　5. で

③ わたし____おかあさんはげんきです。 My mother is fine.

1. は　　　　2. に　　3. を　　4. の　　5. で

④ としょかん____ほんをよみます。 I read books at the library.

1. は　　　　2. に　　3. へ　　4. の　　5. で

⑤ バス____ニューヨークへいきます。 I am going to New York by bus.

1. は　　　　2. で　　3. へ　　4. の　　5. を

Practice 3: 空白を埋めよう。

Fill in the blank spaces with the correct particle.

①　このくるま＿＿＿たかいです。　This car is expensive.

②　わたし＿＿＿としょかん＿＿＿いきます。　I'm going to the library.

③　トムはにちようび＿＿＿まんが＿＿＿よみます。Tom read a comic book on Sunday.

④　わたし＿＿＿日本＿＿＿すんでいます。　I live in Japan.

⑤　どようび＿＿＿やきゅう＿＿＿します。　I am going to play baseball on Saturday.

Practice 4: 正しい形容詞を空白にいれよう。

Fill in the blank spaces with an adjective.

①　Chicago is cold.
シカゴは＿＿＿＿＿＿＿＿＿＿です。

②　Japanese is not easy.
にほんごは＿＿＿＿＿＿＿＿＿＿です。

③　This movie is funny.
このえいがは＿＿＿＿＿＿＿＿＿です。

④　I am going to eat a tasty pizza.
＿＿＿＿＿＿＿＿ピザをたべます。

⑤　This camera isn't expensive.
このカメラは＿＿＿＿＿＿＿＿＿です。

⑥　This test is not difficult.
テストは＿＿＿＿＿＿＿＿＿＿です。

⑦　What is your favorite food?
＿＿＿＿＿＿＿＿たべものはなんですか？

⑧　I'm busy today.
きょうは＿＿＿＿＿＿＿＿＿＿です。

Practice 5: 日本語で書いてみよう。

Below you will find a list of words and pictures; use these to create short sentences in Japanese.

Example: Coffee		I drink coffee. コーヒーをのみます
① Hamburger		
② School		

③ Book		
④ Japanese		
⑤ Soccer		
⑥ Music		
⑦ English		

Listening and Speaking

Practice 1: 音声をきいて、空白を埋めよう。📢

Four students are talking about what they will do this weekend. Listen to the audio and answer the questions.

どようびは _____ をみます。
にちようびは _____ をします。

ネルソン

1. What is Nelson going to watch on Saturday?

①アニメ　②にほんごのテレビ　③えいが　④アメリカのドラマ　⑤バスケットボール

2. What is Nelson going to do on Sunday?

①テニス　②スキー　③バスケットボール　④やきゅう　⑤バレーボール

どようびは _____。
にちようびは _____。

フアン

1. Where is Juan going on Saturday?

①かいもの　②えいがかん　③としょかん　④りょうがえじょ　⑤ぎんこう

2. Where is Juan going on Sunday?

①パラグアイ　②がっこう　③トイレ　④日本　⑤はくぶつかん

アラダ

どようびは＿＿＿＿＿。
にちようびは＿＿＿＿＿をみます。

1. What is Arada going to do on Saturday?　Make sure the answer is in hiragana and katakana.

_____

2. What is Arada going to watch on Sunday?
①テレビ　②えいが　③オペラ　④やきゅう　⑤サッカー

リサ

どようびは＿＿＿＿にいきます。
にちようびはいえで＿＿＿＿＿。

1. Where is Lisa going on Saturday?
①げんこう　②レストラン　③コーヒーショップ　④りょうがえじょ　⑤がっこう
2. What is Lisa going to do on Sunday?　Make sure the answer is in hiragana and katakana.

ソア

どようびは＿＿＿＿＿＿。
にちようびは＿＿＿＿＿。

1. What is Soah going to do on Saturday?
① Shop　② Going to a restaurant　③ Cook　④ Work　⑤ Study
2. What is Soah going to do on Sunday?　Make sure the answer is in hiragana and katakana.

_____

Part 3: 自己紹介 Introduce Yourself in Japanese
<ruby>自己紹介<rt>じこしょうかい</rt></ruby>

Imagine meeting someone for the first time in Japan. Here are some possible questions they may ask. Listen to the audio and practice how to answer the questions, using answers that are provided.

> 📢 Question 1: What is your name?
> おなまえはなんですか？

Possible answers:

わたしのなまえは<u>ジョン</u>です。 My name is <u>John.</u>

<u>ジョン</u>です。 I'm <u>John.</u>

> 📢 Question 2: Where are you from?
> しゅっしんはどこですか？

Possible answers:

<u>アメリカのシカゴ</u>です。 I'm from <u>the United States, from the city of Chicago</u>.

<u>アメリカのシカゴ</u>からきました。 I came from <u>the United States, from the city of Chicago.</u>

<u>アメリカ人</u>です。 I'm <u>American</u>.

> 📢 Question 3: Where do you live?
> どこにすんでいますか？

Possible answer:

<u>とうきょう</u>にすんでいます。 I live in <u>Tokyo</u>.

📢 Question 4: What do you do in Japan?
日本でなにをしているんですか？

Possible answer:

にほんごをべんきょうしています。 I am studying Japanese.

Subjects

れきし（歴史） history	にほんご（日本語） Japanese
けいざい（経済） economics	コンピューター computers
せいじ（政治） politics	すうがく（数学） mathematics
ビジネス business	かがく（科学）science

ぎんこうではたらいています。 I work for the bank.

わたしはえいごのせんせいです。 I am an English teacher.

Occupations

かいしゃいん（会社員） company employee	べんごし（弁護士） lawyer
いしゃ（医者） doctor	ちょうりし（調理師） chef
かんごし（看護師） nurse	ジャーナリスト journalist
だいく（大工） carpenter	こうむいん（公務員） government worker

📢 Question 5: What are your hobbies?
しゅみはなんですか？

Possible answers:

バスケットボールがだいすきです。 I love basketball.

しゅみはバスケットボールです。 I play basketball as a hobby.

Practice 1: 音声をきいて、答えをえらぼう。📢

Ken and a foreign exchange student are having conversation. Listen to their conversation and answer the questions below.

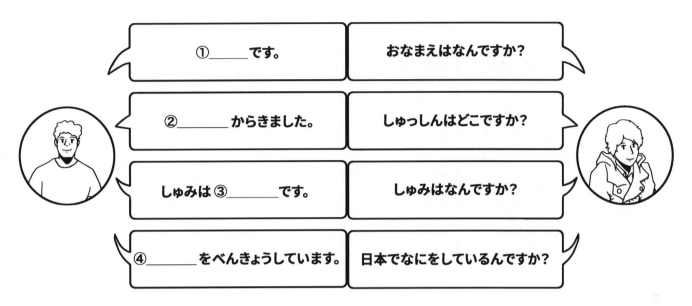

① What is the foreign exchange student's name?
1. ダニエル   2. フアン   3. トム   4. ホセ   5. アラン

② Where is he from?
1. メキシコ   2. アメリカ   3. パラグアイ   4. アルゼンチン   5. ベトナム

③ What are his hobbies?
1. サッカー   2. バレーボール   3. ゲーム   4. べんきょう   5. スキー

④ What is he studying in Japan?
1. すうがく   2. ビジネス   3. ゲーム   4. コンピューター   5. れきし

Practice 2: 自己紹介を読んで、質問に答えよう。

Arada is introducing herself. Read what she says and answer the questions that follow.

アラダ

わたしのなまえはアラダです。

2019ねんにインドからきました。

いまはとうきょうにすんでいます。

日本で、にほんごとけいざいをべんきょうしています。

しゅみはゲームです。すきなたべものはケーキです。

どうぞよろしくおねがいします。

1. Where is Arada from?
   ①アメリカ　②メキシコ　③とうきょう　④インド　⑤タイ

2. What is she studying in Japan? Select all of her subjects.
   ①えいご　②ゲーム　③にほんご　④けいざい　⑤とうきょう

3. What are her hobbies?
   ①インド　②ゲーム　③とうきょう　④アラダ　⑤ケーキ

4. What is her favorite food?
   ①インド　②ゲーム　③とうきょう　④ケーキ　⑤けいざい

Practice 3: 自己紹介文を書いてみよう。

Read the example and write your own introduction.

自己紹介 **Introduction of self**

わたしのなまえはシンジです。
My name is Shinji.
日本人です。でも、いまはパラグアイにすんでいます。
I'm Japanese, but I live in Paraguay.
かがくをべんきょうしています。
I am studying science.
バスケットボールがだいすきです。
I love playing basketball.
どうぞよろしくおねがいします。
Nice to meet you!

自己紹介 **Introduction of Self**

わたしのなまえは＿＿＿＿＿＿＿＿です。
　　　　　　　　　　　　Name
＿＿＿＿＿＿＿人です。いまは、＿＿＿＿＿＿＿にすんでいます。
　Nationality　　　　　　　　*Where you live*

＿＿＿＿＿＿＿＿＿＿＿＿＿＿＿＿＿＿＿。
What do you do? ↗

＿＿＿＿＿＿＿＿＿＿＿＿＿＿＿＿＿＿＿。
What are your hobbies? ↗

どうぞよろしくおねがいします。

単語リスト：List of Japanese Vocabulary
This is all the vocabulary you have learned in this lesson:

Verbs
たべる：to eat
おきる：to get up
ねる：to go to bed
みる：to watch, to see
おしえる：to teach
いく：to go
かえる：to go home
きく：to listen
のむ：to drink
はなす：to speak
よむ：to read
はたらく：to work
べんきょうする：to study
する：to do, to play (sport)
くる：to come
すむ：to live

Adjectives
あつい：hot
さむい ：cold
おもしろい：interesting, funny
いそがしい：busy
たかい：expensive
やすい：cheap
おいしい：tasty
むずかしい：difficult
げんきな：healthy
しずかな：quiet
きれいな：beautiful
すきな：favorite
かんたんな：easy

Nouns
あめ：rain
がくせい：student
きょう：today
しゅみ：hobby
れきし：history
にほんご：Japanese
けいざい：economics
コンピューター：computer
せいじ：politics
すうがく：mathematics
ビジネス： business
かがく：science
かいしゃいん：company employee
べんごし：lawyer
いしゃ：doctor
ちょうりし：chef
かんごし：nurse
ジャーナリスト：journalist
だいく：carpenter
こうむいん：government worker

Conclusion

Congratulations on finishing this book! You have completed the first step of learning Japanese. Learning hiragana and katakana is one of the most important parts of your journey. Since Japanese has such a unique writing system and the grammar is very different from English, it must have taken some time and energy for you to complete this book. We commend you again for your effort and perseverance.

Having finished this book, you are now able to read and write two of the three sets of characters in Japanese: hiragana and katakana. What a great advantage for you! Having completed this book, here is a summary of some of the skills that you have learned and here is how you can use some of them. You can now confidently read the menu at any Japanese restaurant. You are now able to go shopping at any Japanese store. If you get lost, you have the skill sets to successfully ask for directions and find your way to your destination. More importantly, this book has helped you acquire the skill sets to make friends by introducing yourself and explaining your likes and dislikes.

We are certain that after putting in all that work, you do not want to forget what you have accomplished with this book. Here are three pro tips to help you remember what you have already learned in this book.

1. Review *Japanese Hiragana and Katakana Made Easy*

We encourage you to review this book from time to time to remind yourself of what you have learned. Use the lists of the Japanese vocabulary pages to review all new vocabulary you learned in each chapter. You can use lesson 7 to review all the basic Japanese grammar, which will help you form more sentences instead of memorizing hundreds of Japanese words.

2. Make good use of the audio sections

Use the hiragana and katakana charts to get familiar with all the pronunciation of characters you cannot pronounce correctly. We encourage you to listen repeatedly to all audio recordings in this book to get used to the Japanese sounds.

3. Practice reading hiragana and katakana in real-life

If you are visiting Japan, you will find hiragana and katakana everywhere. Try to read these characters aloud and use a dictionary to make sure of the meaning of new vocabulary and record it. Even if you are not in Japan, look for opportunities where you can listen and read hiragana and katakana scripts and audio, for example, YouTube, Netflix and other social media platforms. Having completed this book, you will be surprised how much Japanese content you can read.

Once again, well done for getting this far. In Japanese we say "おめでとうございます." We as the writers and publishers of this book are proud of your accomplishments. But your journey is not over yet. As you already know, Japanese has three sets of characters. In this book, we have only covered two sets. The missing set is Kanji. With you in mind we have prepared user-friendly kanji book that we know you will love. That is why we encourage you to continue your language journey with us.

解答：Answer Key

Lesson 1

Part 2: Practice

Reading and Writing
Practice 2
1) ② か
2) ② も
3) ⑤ し
4) ① つ
5) ③ て
6) ④ ね
7) ④ の
8) ② れ
9) ③ そ
10) ③ を
11) ① き
12) ③ ぬ
13) ⑤ ら
14) ③ と
15) ② ふ
16) ④ ち
17) ⑤ や
18) ① せ
19) ① く
20) ② ほ

Listening and Speaking
Practice 1
1. ③ かさ
2. ② ふく
3. ③ はな
4. ① あめ
5. ④ ほし
6. ③ くるま
7. ④ おんな

Practice 2
1. たいよう
2. あつい
3. さむい
4. つき
5. よる
6. みかん
7. ちかてつ
8. えき
9. くうこう
10. けいさつ
11. にほん

Part 3: Vocabulary
Practice 1
① はさみ
② さいふ
③ おかし
④ おさら
⑤ とけい
⑥ え
⑦ いす
⑧ かみ
⑨ ほん
⑩ つくえ

Lesson 2

Part 2: Practice

Reading and Writing
Practice 2
1) ⑤ ぎ
2) ① ざ
3) ② で
4) ③ ぶ
5) ④ ぺ
6) ① ぐ
7) ⑤ ぜ
8) ③ ど
9) ④ ぷ
1 0) ② が

Listening and Speaking
Practice 1
1. かぎ
2. おじぎ
3. でんき
4. みず
5. しんぶん
6. どろぼう
7. えんぴつ

Practice 2
1. どうぶつ
2. おんがく
3. だいがく
4. べんごし
5. いそがしい

Part 3: Vocabulary
Practice 1
あたま：head
め：eye
うで：arm
おなか：stomach
て：hand
ゆび：finger
かみ（のけ）：hair
みみ：ear
はな：nose
かた：shoulder
ひざ：knee
あし：foot, leg

Part 4: Greeting in Japanese
Practice 2
1）おはようございます
2）ただいま
3）はじめまして
4）ごちそうさまでした
5）よろしくおねがいします

Practice 3
1）おはよう
2）こんばんは
3）すみません
4）いただきます
5）よろしくおねがいします

Lesson 3

Part 2: Practice
Practice 2
1) ③みゅ
2) ②ぴゅ
3) ④きょ
4) ①ぎゃ
5) ②びゃ
6) ③ひゃ
7) ②しゃ
8) ⑤にゃ
9) ④きゃ
１０) ③じょ

Practice 3
しゅくだい：Homework
やきゅう：Baseball
おちゃ：Tea
じゅぎょう：Class, Lesson
もくひょう：Goal
きって：Stamp

Listening and Speaking
Practice 1
1. ③らいしゅう
2. ④きっぷ
3. ②でんしゃ
4. ③れんしゅう
5. ①うちゅう

Practice 2
1. しょうゆ
2. じゃがいも
3. ばった
4. きんぎょ

5. とうきょう
6. かぼちゃ
7. きゅうり
8. きょうだい
9. しゃしん

Part 3: Vocabulary
Practice 1
①とり
②くじゃく
③ひょう
④くま
⑤いぬ
⑥ねずみ
⑦ねこ
⑧かえる
⑨へび
⑩うま
⑪うし
⑫さる

Part 4: Where is…?
Practice 1
①としょかん
②がっこう
③けいさつしょ
④ぎんこう
⑤ゆうびんきょく
⑥びょういん
⑦りょうがえじょ
⑧といれ

Practice 2
1. としょかんはどこですか
2. けいさつしょはどこですか
3. がっこうはどこですか
4. ぎんこうはどこですか
5. ゆうびんきょくはどこですか
6. びょういんはどこですか
7. りょうがえじょはどこですか
8. といれはどこですか

Part 5: Numbers and Price
Practice 2
① 8
② 3 0
③ 2 0 0 0
④ 8 0 0 0
⑤ 6 0 0
⑥ 2 0 2 0
⑦ 7 0 0 0 0
⑧ 9 0 0 0 0
⑨ 8 9 0 0 0
⑩ 3 0 0

Practice 3
1. A: この（　ほん　）はいくらですか？
   B:（　５００　）円です。
2. A: この（はさみ）はいくらですか？
   B:（　２００　）円です。
3. A: この（　くつ　）はいくらですか？
   B:（　７０００　）円です。
4. A: この（えんぴつ）はいくらですか？
   B:（　１５０　）円です。
5. A: この（ぼうし）はいくらですか？
   B:（　２０００　）円です。
6. A: この（かさ）はいくらですか？
   B:（　４５０　）円です。

Lesson 4

Part 2: Practice
Reading and Writing
Practice 2
1)②キ
2)③サ
3)①テ
4)④ナ
5)⑤ホ
6)②メ
7)①ヨ
8)②ラ
9)④ケ
10)⑤ス
11)③ツ
12)①ノ
13)③ヒ
14)④モ
15)⑤ヤ
16)①ル
17)②ワ
18)⑤カ
19)①ネ
10)③ト

Listening and Speaking
Practice 1
1)①レタス
2)③トマト
3)②メロン
4)①ワイン
5)①コメント
6)③テスト
7)④クラス
8)②リスク
9)②アニメ
10)③トイレ

Practice 2
①オンライン
②カメラマン
③トンネル
④ハンカチ
⑤クリスマス
⑥マラソン
⑦キス
⑧アメリカ
⑨リサイクル
⑩レストラン

Lesson 5

Part 2: Practice
Reading and Writing
Practice 1
1）⑤グ
2）②ジ
3）④デ
4）①ボ
5）②パ
6）③ガ
7）③ゾ
8）⑤ド
9）①ピ
１０）②ゴ

Listening and Speaking
Practice 1
①アルバム
②ポスト
③ビジネス
④サプリメント
⑤ボタン
⑥ガソリンスタンド
⑦パイプ
⑧エンジニア
⑨アルバイト
⑩ビザ
⑪ダイヤモンド
⑫イグアナ
⑬カブトムシ
⑭パンダ
⑮ザリガニ

Part 4: Where are you from?
Practice 2
Hiroko：にほん
Sarah：イギリス
Noa：みなみアフリカ

Practice 3
①かんこく
②みなみアフリカ
③インド
④フランス
⑤にほん
⑥ナイジェリア
⑦パラグアイ
⑧アメリカ

Lesson 6

Part 2: Practice
Reading and Writing
Practice 2
1) ③キュ
2) ①シャ
3) ②ニャ
4) ③ヒョ
5) ⑤ミャ
6) ③リャ
7) ①ギョ
8) ⑤ビャ
9) ①ピュ
10) ①ジュ
11) ②キャ
12) ④ビョ
13) ①リュ
14) ②ディ
15) ⑤フィ
16) ④ヴァ
17) ②ジェ
18) ③イェ

Practice 3
ギター：guitar
ゲーム：game
キャンプ：camp
シャワー：shower
コーヒーショップ：coffee shop, cafe
チケット：ticket
オリンピック：Olympics
ジャケット：jacket

Listening and Speaking
Practice 1
1.③シャツ
2.④ニュース
3.①アパート
4.②コーヒー
5.④ジーンズ

Practice 2
①ファイル
②スープ
③サーフィン
④ソファー
⑤テーブル
⑥コンピューター
⑦トラック
⑧チーズ
⑨バター
⑩プラスチック
⑪ボール
⑫ボール
⑬チェス

Part 3: Vocabulary
Practice 1
プリンター：printer
ラジオ：radio
マウス：mouse
タブレット：tablet
スマホ（スマートフォン）：smartphone
モデム：modem
インターネット：Internet
キーボード：keyboard
カメラ：camera
パソコン：PC

Practice 2
テニス：tennis
アイスホッケー：ice hockey
やきゅう：baseball
バレーボール：volleyball
バスケットボール：basketball
サッカー：soccer
スキー：ski
ラグビー：rugby
ゴルフ：golf

Part 4: How to order food in a restaurant
Practice 1
Lunch
①サンドイッチ
②ホットドック
③ラーメン
④ハンバーガー
⑤フライドポテト
⑥タコス
Dinner
①ピザ
②スパゲッティ
③カレーライス
④サラダ
⑤クリームシチュー
⑥ステーキ
Dessert
①クッキー
②アイスクリーム
③ソフトクリーム
④チョコレートケーキ
⑤ドーナッツ

Drink
①オレンジジュース
②アップルジュース
③コーヒー
④カプチーノ
⑤カフェラテ

Practice 2
①サンドイッチをみっつおねがいします。
②アイスクリームをふたつおねがいします。
③アップルジュースをひとつおねがいします。
④ピザをひとつ、ハンバーガーをひとつおねがいします。

Practice 3
①ビーフステーキとカプチーノ
②カレーライス、サラダ、カフェラテ
③２８００えん

Part 5: What is this?
Practice 1
①タブレット
②キーボード
③タコス
④ハンバーガー

Part 6: Things that you like and things that you don't like
Practice 1
①すし　Sushi
②バスケットボール　Basketball
③ラーメン　Ramen

Lesson 7

Part 2: Practice
Reading and Writing
Practice 1
①False
②True
③True
④False
⑤True

Practice 2
①   2. に
②   3. を
③   4. の
④   5. で
⑤   2. で

Practice 3
①このくるまはたかいです。
②わたしはとしょかんにいきます。
③トムはにちようびにまんがをよみます。
④わたしは日本にすんでいます。
⑤どようびにやきゅうをします。

Practice 4
①シカゴはさむいです。
②にほんごはかんたんじゃないです。
③このえいがはおもしろいです。
④おいしいピザをたべます。
⑤このカメラはたかくないです。
⑥テストはむずかしくないです。
⑦すきなたべものはなんですか?
⑧きょうはいそがしいです。

Practice 5
①ハンバーガーをたべます
②がっこうにいきます

③ほんをよみます
④にほんごをべんきょうします
⑤サッカーをします
⑥おんがくをききます
⑦えいごをはなします

Listening and Speaking
Practice 1
ネルソン
1. ②にほんごのテレビ
2. ①テニス
フアン
1. ①かいもの
2. ⑤はくぶつかん
アラダ
1. こうえんにいきます。
2. ④やきゅう
リサ
1. ②レストラン
2. いえでえいがをみます。
ソア
1. ④Work / はたらきます。
2. ゲームをします。

Part 3: Introduce yourself in Japanese
Practice 1
①   1. ダニエル
②   1. メキシコ
③   1. サッカー
④   4. コンピューター
Practice 2
1. ④インド
2. ③にほんご　④けいざい
3. ②ゲーム
4. ④ケーキ

MORE BOOKS BY LINGO MASTERY

We are not done teaching you Japanese until you're fluent!

Here are some other titles you might find useful in your journey of mastering Japanese:

- ✅ Japanese Short Stories for Beginners
- ✅ Intermediate Japanese Short Stories
- ✅ 2000 Most Common Japanese Words in Context
- ✅ Conversational Japanese Dialogues

But we got many more!

Check out all of our titles at **www.LingoMastery.com/japanese**

Made in the USA
Las Vegas, NV
04 August 2023

75635039R00109